Healed
FROM CANCER TO SURVIVA
A JOURNEY THAT INSPIRED ALL

WRITTEN & CREATED BY
EVELINA JOHNSON BUENDIA

Published by BlackGold Publishing, LLC in partnership with The BlackGold Book League of Hampton Roads.

1706 Todds Lane, Suite 258
Hampton, VA 23666

Edited by Noelle B.
Designed by Evelina Johnson Buendia
Cover Photo by Jeanita R. Castille
Copyright © 2023 by Evelina Johnson Buendia
All rights reserved.
No part of this book may be reproduced, scanned, or distributed in any printed or electronic form without permission.
Printed in the United States of America

Advance Praise For
Healed: From Cancer To Surviva

"If ever there was an inspirational story, this is it. I've known Evelina for many years, and I've watched her face many adversities. However, her journey through breast cancer and the loss of her father has not only shown me her strength, but it has shown me faith like I've never seen. If you want to see faithful victory in action, this is the book for you!"
— Catina Burrell

"You have a special gift. Writing. Not only was this cathartic for you, but you also allowed your followers to experience the encouragement and highs and lows of being human. You have given a sense of victory to those who have to follow in your shoes. Your words jump off the page to your readers. They will become a part of Oprah's Book Club reading!"
— Mrs. V

"You inspire me to be better than what I am and your strength is contagious. With everything that you have been through, I don't know how you stayed so strong? I look at you and want to grow up to be just like you. What can I say? Your faith in the Lord is so strong that you never gave it a second thought that you would be healed. You are one of the strongest people I know and never change who you are."
— Deborah McLaurin

Advance Praise For
Healed: From Cancer To Surviva

"You have been a tremendous blessing to me; from the moment we met. You flourished in the things of God and remained obedient to God's call on your life, and because of that, it resulted in being your best self (God's best!). This carried over into every aspect of your life despite the challenges you faced but endured. My sister, you have been blessed to be a blessing through sharing the most trying times in your life, which birthed your blog. Your blog not only blessed me but invited me into your world intimately. I was honored that you chose to share your journey with me. In my heart, I journeyed with you emotionally and spiritually as you demonstrated God's miraculous power and His ability to comfort, strengthen, and heal you. God used you through your blog to increase my faith, prayer life, and sustainability. Your tenacity and strength have helped so many people, and will continue to help others as God get the glory."

- Martha Jones

~ I Dedicate... ~

While drafting this book, I realized that the one person who has been my rock through it all never got enough credit. It's no wonder why people often ask me, "You talk so much about your father, but is your mother still around?" And the answer to that is yes, she's still around. In fact, from day one, she never left my side. I've just always been so much of a daddy's girl because I look up to him in so many ways. However, my mama never left my side. Every treatment she was there; every home-cooked meal, she made it; Emil, she took care of him! In fact, truth be told, he's really her baby! She was there for **EVERYTHING**!! And always has been. That's why if this book should be dedicated to anyone, it should be devoted to her, for the Lord blessed us with a mother who doesn't get all the credit she deserves. A woman that, when I think about it, was made specifically by God, with the sole purpose of being a "Mother."

Thank you, Mami, for always taking care of me. Te amo.
....
To my father, for being my biggest cheerleader.
....
To my baby boy Emil, for coming into my life in God's perfect timing.
...
To "Mi Familia," for **NEVER** leaving my side.

I Dedicate...

To Sashi, my daughter, for choosing to love me.

….

To my 80%, for your encouragement, love and support.

….

To MyLifeLine.org for giving me a platform to share my "**GIFT**."

…..

To my LINAIMAGING family, for your love, patience and understanding.

…..

To the Riverside Cancer Center for walking with me **EVERY** step of the way.

….

To the next Survival! For allowing me to encourage you in **THE FIGHT**.

….

To my Heavenly Father, for using me, stretching me and molding me.

I love you all.

Preface

The idea of recording one of my most intimate faith journeys with God was never my intention. Then again, the Bible surely tells us that, His thoughts are not our thoughts and our ways are not His ways. (Isaiah 55:8 NIV)

Healed: From Cancer to Surviva, A Journey That Inspired All, is perhaps one of **THE** greatest callings upon my life. For throughout my entire journey, God used my gift of writing not only as a source of comfort for me but as a way of "using me." (Isaiah 6:8 NIV)

For I wrote from beginning to end, read to every single person God sent my way, and I believed in every word that was written, and as a result, I was, **HEALED**.

Friends, my heart's desire is for my journey to encourage the next **SURVIVA** to walk confidently in her healing…knowing that the Lord will never leave her nor forsake her. (Hebrews 13:5 ESV) And my prayer is also that this **FAITH** walk will encourage **EVERYONE** else to just keep on looking **UP**.

For God is able to do **ALL** things, **ALL** things if we only **CHOOSE TO BELIEVE**. (Mark 9:23 NIV)

Preface

So let me ask you, are you up for the challenge?
Are you prepared to experience His goodness?
Are you ready to go all in?

Whether hesitant or not, journey with me from Cancer to Surviva. An experience that will leave you with no other choice, **BUT**... to **BELIEVE**!

Amen. Be Encouraged.

Love, Lina

Introduction
JULY 11, 2017

"Miss Johnson, your biopsy shows that the three spots that we've tested are positive for **Breast Cancer.**"

Yeah, I know, I couldn't believe it myself. But just like I told my doctor, I know that no matter what, **"GOD's GOT ME."** He healed me when I was hit by a car, and He healed me when I needed a blood transfusion. He healed me then and I know that He'll heal me now.

Yeah, I can't lie; the first couple of days before the biopsy were tough on me and now, after the confirmation, it's even harder. I've asked God, "why me?" And He's responded, "Evelina, why not you? You're strong, you're a survivor and you look up to me and I know that when I heal you, you'll testify to my goodness and encourage so many others. So again, I say why not you?" Therefore, I must trust God, no matter how bad this sounds, because I know that as I'm writing this, I'm already being healed.

DO YOU KNOW THE STAGE?

No, and honestly, once they confirm that, I don't wanna know either. Why not?? Because I don't want anything to become a stumbling block to my faith. It's bad enough knowing that it's Cancer. And for many people, Cancer = death. But I've discovered that Cancer is not a death sentence at all; but rather a **LIFE** sentence because it pushes one to live and **I CAN-CER VIVE** this!

Therefore, I'm declaring from this day forward that "**I'M HEALED** and **I'M SAVED**!" Friends, there's **POWER** in **SPOKEN WORDS**. I myself know that to be a fact. In 2001 I said, "Ima walk!" and I walked. Another time I said I wanted my first car to be a "Honda Civic EX," and doggone it I was not driving off that lot without what I wanted :) Lol. So I say, **SPEAK UP**!

WHAT I KNOW NOW

My genetics results came out negative!!! Therefore, I'm not at high risk for any other Cancers in the future, and a mastectomy is not necessary.

The Cancer is ER/PR + Her2 (-). From my understanding, that means this form of Cancer usually responds well to treatment.

Lord willing, if the rest of my test results come out well, I'll be starting treatment in August (20 weeks of chemo).

After chemo, I'll decide on my surgical procedure (lumpectomy, mastectomy, or unilateral).

WHAT I NEED FROM YOU

POSITIVE THINKING! This journey won't be easy, so I'm asking all of you to please continue to encourage me at all times. Nothing is impossible for God; He will save me! So don't even entertain any negative thoughts because how else will you be able to uplift me? God works in miraculous ways; in all honesty, I could go in tomorrow for testing, and it may not even be there anymore.

> "Whatever, we know that can't happen, Evelina!"

Okay, y'all keep putting God in a box if you want to cause my God is greater than Cancer or any other disease. He's supernatural!

The Journey Begins

SUNDAY, JULY 30

I Trust Him

Today in church, I had to ask myself, "How is it that I can stand before the altar and not shed a tear?"

It's because my faith is deeply rooted in my healer. He knows that I'm all cried out and trusting Him with my life. He knows that this battle is His and not mine. He knows that I've already prophesied that "I am a survivor," He knows that I have enough **WORD** in me to trust in Him. He knows that I am surrounded by prayer warriors and He knows that I've experienced His saving grace. So yes, I stood without shedding a tear today, but it's only because this load is just too heavy for me to carry, and I'm learning what it truly means to **LET GO** and **LET GOD**.

Be still. Let go and let God.
Psalm 46:10

MONDAY, JULY 31

Testimonies

Tonight, without knowing my situation, a young pastor hugged me and whispered in my ear, "There once was a woman who was given 45 days to live; the doctors sent her home claiming that there was nothing more that **THEY** could do for her. While at home, waiting to die, she became pregnant, and today that baby boy is encouraging you."

It's amazing how God uses other people to bless you.

#mygodisawesome #nothingsimpossible #ourhealer #thankyoujesus #amazingtestimony #godhasthefinalsay

TUESDAY, AUGUST 1
Solid Rock

"Did this storm catch you on rock or sand?" If you're on a solid rock, the wind and rain may pound against your house, but your foundation will stand up against each and every blow this Cancer tries to deliver. If the ground beneath you is shaky, take heart!" - Grace for Each Hour: Through the Breast Cancer Journey by Nelson, Mary J.

Friends, I'm so thankful that I know the Lord; I can't even imagine going through this season **LOST** and depressed. It feels like my strength is renewed each day, and even my doctors see a **SHIFT** in me. My oncologist said, "It's okay if you cried last week; you needed to!" and My surgeon was so happy that my vocabulary is changing from "**WHAT IF**s" to proclaiming **VICTORY**. (He's a sweetheart. Actually, both of them are, but I can truly tell that he loves the Lord.)

WHAT HAPPENED TODAY?

- * My echo results came out perfect!!! One test down, three more to go. **AMEN**!
- * Scheduled my **CHEMO PORT** surgery for the 10th (outpatient).
- * I'll start chemo on the 18th @ 10 am.

WHAT'S NEXT?

Tomorrow:

- * Chemo Overview Class
- * Brain Scan
- * Lab Work for my Port Surgery

HOW ARE YOU FEELING?

Like I said earlier, God's in control, and I'm already being **HEALED**. It's because of Him and only Him that I can smile and be happy today, for I am blessed with a team of great doctors: Dr. K and Dr. C.

WEDNESDAY, AUGUST 2

Support System

I just wanted to take this moment to brag about my "**CIRCLE**." Here is just a snippet of all the love and support that I've been given. I Love You All.

"Praise God! Your faith has made you whole!!! I will not only pray for you but with you. I stand in total agreement that you are healed. I love you and am here for whatever you need! Your message is a true inspiration to me. Keep your faith, Evelina; it will carry you through every test along this journey. God is good!!!"

"I'm not worried about you AT ALL! Because I KNOOOOOW you are gonna be just fine! This too shall pass, and you will be better because of this experience! TRUST GOD and leave everything up to Him! I really want to walk this walk with you every step of the way! God is a healer, and he is healing you as I type! AMEN!! I'm here to help support you and also to answer any questions!! Again I'm not worried about you at all because like my beautiful sister used to always say, "God's got you boo!"

"...You are so brave! I'm so proud of you. This would have crushed some people, but not you. You are a fighter and will conquer it. We are right here for you."

"Evelina!!! You know I am already praying for you and declaring your healing in this life! On this Earth! Long-life! I am here! All the way!!! I stand in agreement with you that you shall live and not die and declare the works of the Lord!"

"God is good friend...please just stay strong, don't think about anything except for what you need to do to be there for your little man. Pray often and maintain an attitude of gratitude only! Remove negative people and habits from your life and only stay in the moment. Do not think about the past or the future but the here and now."

Special thanks to my "Survivor Sister" Tracey for attending my chemo class with me today. Praise God for sending me someone who knows exactly what I'm going through from day to day. I love you.

> *"As iron sharpens iron, so one person sharpens another."*
> Proverbs 27:17 NIV

THURSDAY, AUGUST 3
Reflections

Lately, I've been a little exhausted going from appointment to appointment, whether it's seeing a doctor, getting lab work, or some other tests for preparation. That at times in the waiting room, I just stop to think, "What if I would've just prayed?"

You see, my concern with my breast started after a surgical procedure I had several years ago when the surgeon said to me, "I removed what I had to remove, but I saw some other things in there, but I just left them alone." And I remember thinking "what do you mean you just left it alone???" but I guess he figured since what he took out was benign surely the rest had to be and perhaps, it was. But ever since then, what he said, just always stayed on my mind.

Then I can't remember how much longer after that. Every now and then, my breast would leak a sticky fluid. Of course,

I would mention it to my doctors, but they never saw it as a big concern. To them, it was just scar tissue or my body undergoing life changes. Cause for one, I was young and secondly, I wasn't considered at high risk even though I had a paternal aunt who had passed away from breast cancer.

So months passed and the same thing would happen, but this time it dripped a tinge of blood, and I just knew that wasn't right. At that point, I had one ultrasound, and it revealed that nothing was going on. But the last appointment I had, I regretted it because I almost did have a mammogram, but because of my fear of it hurting, based on the many horror stories I've heard, I told the nurse, "**NOOO** it's gonna hurt, I don't want them to squish my titties" lol, and she said "Oh it's okay you don't need it anyway because you're young and you're not at high risk." So again, they did an ultrasound, but this time I remember the nurse saying out loud, "I see something," and the doctor said, "no, it's nothing, that's just her breast getting ready to produce milk" (because I'm of childbearing age).

At that point, I said, "You know what, they said it's nothing, and I'm just going to leave it alone."

But today, I can't help but wonder, "What if I would've stopped and prayed?" What if I would've left this in the hands of the Lord and said, "Father, please heal my body."

Just like the Pastor mentioned last week, oftentimes, what should be our first step is our last resort. And that is sooo true cause instead of looking up, I just said, "Whatever," and stayed with that worry deep inside of me.

My surgeon says, "We can't think about the past and what they said or didn't do; at your age if it was anything, it's often difficult to determine what's what." But still, I can't help but to think about how different my story would've been if I had just stopped and prayed.

Therefore, friends, I encourage you today to take a moment and "look up." Regardless of what you're going through, know that God can heal you and deliver you from that storm. He wants to take that burden off your shoulders; He wants to be the one to take away that worry that bothers you late into the midnight hours. So surrender it all to Him and watch your situation begin to turn around.

Love you all.

"If you have time to worry, you have time to pray."
Author Unknown

FRIDAY, AUGUST 4

Encourage

There's not a day that God hasn't used someone to encourage me. Just this week:

TODAY a bill collector whom I'd usually send straight to voicemail said, "Trust God, stay positive, be strong and fight!"

YESTERDAY the American Cancer Society Administrator said, "I believe everything happens for a reason, and God is going to use you."

WEDNESDAY, a Cancer survivor said, "I pass on to you the peace that surpasses all understanding."

TUESDAY, another survivor said, "Everything is going to be fine."

MONDAY, the author of my devotional reminded me to stand on Solid Rock.

#ENCOURAGE someone today!

SUNDAY, AUGUST 6
Let's Be Real

My devotional last night was titled "Let's Be Real," where the author talks about how difficult it is to come to terms with your diagnosis when you call it anything other than its name.

And she's absolutely right. Yesterday after breaking the news to a friend, he looked at me and said, "You're kidding me, right? How can you say that you have Cancer and just act like it's nothing?" And I said, "Because I trust God, therefore I speak with confidence, knowing that He's going to heal me."

Friends, I just wanna say I ain't no "Super Christian." This confidence didn't just happen overnight. But thank God cause it's Him who renews my strength each and every day.

Heck! Y'all should've heard me just two weeks ago telling my oncologist, "I don't want this infection inside of me!" Notice, I said "infection" and not Cancer cause calling it by its name was just too difficult for me to do without breaking down. And now, look at God. I can speak without shedding a tear.

You see, we've gotta know and understand who we serve. Don't you know we serve a master that is greater than any Cancer?! We serve a master that's a healing doctor, we serve a master who can change any situation around, we serve a master that's above science and best of all we serve a master who's in control. Hallelujah! Therefore, I can't allow Cancer to break me down and **YOU** can't allow your situation to break you down either. I've gotta keep my head up high and say to anyone who questions me, "Yes, I have Cancer, but Cancer doesn't have me. My God is in control and using me for an awesome testimony!"

"Let's Pray: Lord, I don't understand why you've allowed [Evelina] to get Cancer, but you have. I want to believe you're going to use this in a good way, so please help her to speak openly about it. Use her openness to bless others. We Pray, Amen." - Strength Renewed: Meditations for Your Journey Through Breast Cancer by Shirley Corder

P.S. God's about to use your situation too! :)

"All things work together for the good of those who love God."

ROMANS 8:28 GWT

MONDAY, AUGUST 7
Know The Word

I would have to say that I love the waiting room. There's just something special about the strangers you meet, the conversations sparked, the words of encouragement you receive and if you listen closely, oftentimes, God will use these very same people to deliver a word to you.

For instance:

On one occasion while waiting for my full-body scans, a gentleman began to spark a conversation with my father and I. We were talking about the police force and how in this day and age, becoming a police officer is no longer every little boy's dream. So while on the subject, he shares with us a story about his father and how as a farmer, he would always have to deliver crops nearly every day. He also mentioned that although the old man only had an eighth grade education, he was an extremely smart man. Well, check this out, one day, as his father was making a delivery, a young officer pulled him over, claiming that he was in violation of his farming tags. Now, the old man being as smart as he was, said, "no, I'm not, if you would read in **YOUR** manual and turn to chapter so and so, page so and so, paragraph so and so, line so and so you'll see that I'm in no violation." The officer again said, "No sir, you're wrong" and this time the old man says, "do you have your manual? Please take out your manual." The officer, still in disbelief, takes it out and follows the instructions of the old farmer and says, "Wow, well, I guess I've learned something new today!"

Now isn't that amazing, friends!? That officer just knew he had himself a ticket. Lol.

Well, that's the same thing the enemy tries to do to us, and if we're not careful, he'll deceive us. If that farmer had not memorized his rights, he would've been in trouble under false pretense. So it's important for us to not only know the word but to study it for ourselves so that when we're under attack, we can fight the enemy back even harder with the word of God!

Have a Blessed Day. Xoxoxo.

TUESDAY, AUGUST 8
Everything Happens For A Reason

For many years I've always been very big on advocating for Relay for Life or Making Strides. Mainly because I've lost family members to Cancer, one being an aunt who was like a second mother to me. She passed away from the very same Cancer that invaded my body. Breast Cancer.

It was amazing how much support I had from friends, family, and even my coworkers. I remember the first time I started a team within just a few months; we raised a significant amount of money. We were on it! We were so dedicated that my old boss nominated the company to receive an award for our community support. Man, I really miss those days; I kept them so busy that I'm pretty sure they would think to themselves, "Does she have a life?" Lol.

Even the American Cancer Society (ACS) team knew me well, "Hi Evelina!", is what they'd say every time I came to make a donation.

But then, suddenly, my drive for it ended. For some reason, I had this crazy thought that if I kept talking about Cancer so much, I would eventually jinx myself. So I gave it up and shifted my attention elsewhere.

But now look at me, for this time, I'm not walking through those doors to make a deposit today; I'm walking in there today because I declare that I'm a survivor and now, it's just a lil bit more personal. It's about fighting for my life and believing that there's HOPE despite this diagnosis, that one day scientists will discover a cure so that no one else will be affected. It's about being a voice for many who are going through it, giving them the strength that they, too, can make it.

Mrs. Sharon, the Admin Director at ACS, said to me, "I believe everything happens for a reason and you are now being used on a whole 'nother level." And she's so right; many years ago, because of my involvement in Making Strides, I met Tracey, a Breast Cancer survivor who's now become my sister. She's helping me to stay strong every step of the way; in her words, "I wanna be in your back pocket!" lol :) It's amazing how someone who was once a guest speaker of mine became one of my very own caregivers this season.

So it's true, everything does happen for a reason.

WEDNESDAY, AUGUST 9
Incomplete

This morning while getting ready for work, I was reminded of Philippians 1:6, "And I am certain that God, who began the good work within you, will continue His work until it is finally finished on the day when Christ Jesus returns."

Then all of a sudden, I started remembering the t-shirts, pamphlets, ads, tote bags, prayer boxes, and everything I have ever designed to campaign for Breast Cancer.

As I said before, my aunt was like a mother to me, so I really took Breast Cancer awareness to heart.

The scripture tells us that God is a God of completion. Therefore everything that He sees as good, He's sure to help you complete. Meaning that whatever dream **HE** set in you, although delayed, will be completed. So for me God was saying this morning, "Evelina, your work is incomplete."

Even when I reconnect with my college professors, they always say, "oh, I remember you, Evelina! Whatever happened to your Breast Cancer campaign?" and I'd go on to tell 'em how I tried with one company but never got a response. And It's funny to me when they mention that cause I always thought they'd remember me by something else I designed, but nope it was that campaign that made a lasting impression on their hearts.

You see, friends, God wasn't ready for me then; He was only planting the seed. That company may have given me the run around, but God was saying, "no, not yet... I'm going to place you in the right season, with the right people, in the right place, in the right zip code. I'm going to make this campaign even more personal to you so that nobody, I said nobody, will be able to say no to you, my dear. "And look at the opportunity now! Isn't He amazing??? Hallelujah. I went from struggling "on my own" trying to get the right contact # to being in the midst today of one of the top hospitals in Virginia!! I said, isn't He amazing?! Yes!

Don't get me wrong, I'm not happy I endured Cancer to get here; in fact, I wish my suffering on no one. But when you're walking through a storm as I am now, you have to somehow stop and say, "Lord, I know this suffering didn't come from you, but you've allowed it. Therefore, show me what are the things you want me to learn in this season?" And for me, I hear Him saying, "Honey, we must finish what we started."

So friends, if you have a dream, know that God has not forgotten you. Know that it may not have been your season, but God is preparing you for something even greater and mind-blowing. He's preparing to manifest that dream in an atmosphere where nobody, I mean nobody, will be able to say no to you. So continue trusting in Him and believing cause God will not stop until it is "COMPLETE"! Be Encouraged. <3

THURSDAY, AUGUST 10
Courage

"In God, I trust and am not afraid. What can man do to me?"
Psalm 56:11 NIV

LET'S PRAY:

"Lord God, you know [Evelina's] fears. You understand how overwhelming life seems at the moment for her. Help her to keep her eyes on you. She wants to face the future with courage and dignity. Stay real close, Lord, please. Amen."

Strength Renewed: Meditations for Your Journey Through Breast Cancer by Shirley Corder

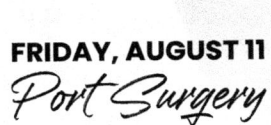

FRIDAY, AUGUST 11
Port Surgery

Thank you all for your continued prayers; my surgery was a complete success, praise God!!!.

Just have some minor aches on my right side where the port was placed, and my throat is a lil sore because they had trouble with the first breathing tube. But other than that, I'm walking in my #healing.

As you can see, they made two incisions. One in my neck and another on my right chest for the device. The marking on the left was just made in the event they couldn't place it on the right.

BUT WHAT EXACTLY IS A PORT EVELINA???

A port is an easier way for the oncologist to administer the chemo by way of one of my main arteries. This way, I'm not being poked in my arms all the time because they say chemo is strong enough to burn you, so my arms are safe now! :)

Love you all <3.

SATURDAY, AUGUST 12
The Hardest Thing To Do

Perhaps the hardest thing I've ever had to do in life was tell my father I have Cancer. He was the first person I thought about when I received my diagnosis. I immediately told the nurse, "I can't tell my father; this will crush him," Especially because I didn't know if his heart could handle it after losing my oldest sister in '05. Not that I thought I would die, but because I know what most people think when hearing the word "Cancer."

But with the help of my mother and sister, I asked him to be strong for me, and the very same man I was worried about said to me as I was crying, "You can't break down because you're going to make it!" He even encouraged me by sharing how he was once diagnosed with a rare case of pneumonia which doctors say most people don't survive. And as his doctors began to share the statistics and the effects of the disease, he told them, "I hear what you're saying, but now I need some time alone to consult my Doctor!" And today, my father is still a walking miracle.

Now, like everyone, I'm pretty sure he has his moments alone when he thinks about my suffering. But he's hanging in there, and it goes to show that you really don't know how strong a person can be until being strong is the only option they have.

HOW ABOUT YOUR MOM AND SISTERS? HOW ARE THEY HOLDING UP?

My mother is doing fine; when she first heard the news, she said, "I'm not even gonna cry cause God's got this." She's watched me battle so many storms in my life that she has no doubt I'll recover soon.

Nita - She's also been encouraging me a lot, and as a matter of fact, she's gonna help me make a halo wig with my own hair!! (Can't wait.)

As for my sisters, they're all in the fight with me.

Praise God for my family; I couldn't have asked for a better support system.

But even so, it still was the hardest thing to do.

SATURDAY, AUGUST 12
There's NO (.)

"Cancer is a word, not a sentence."
IHadCancer.com

SATURDAY, AUGUST 12
Slaying

SUNDAY, AUGUST 13
OMG My Hair!

Buenas! I know some of you are wondering, "Why did she cut her hair? What does that have to do with Cancer? Why do some women go bald? Omg! Her hair was so pretty and long...**OMG! OMG!**

Trust me, yesterday was a lil emotional for me; I can't believe I didn't cry. Even this morning, I couldn't stop thinking about what I did and how real it's becoming. But this is all part of the fight. My original plan was to cut it bald, but then I said let me go short first and go from there.

Hair loss is a side effect of the chemo I'm about to receive. Many Cancer patients don't lose their hair, and I'm guessing it's the type of Cancer or drugs they use to attack their Cancer. It's depressing for sure, having a full head of hair to cutting it because I have to fight for my life. But I'd rather lose it temporarily than refuse chemo. (Believe it or not, some choose their hair over their health.)

When speaking to my survivor sister this morning, she said:

*"Yea, babe, it's gonna fall out. It's just a side effect. You want it to fall out because it means chemo is **DESTROYING** the Cancer! Which is what you want it to do! But it will grow back and you will have your life! And my continued friendship! LOL, what could be better than that!*

Yup! Hairs are like cells, and you want the chemo to destroy **ALL** the cells!!!! Good, bad, and ugly!!! So your body can regenerate good cells in the proper amount!! So hey, if you gotta be bald for a **SHORT** season, then all is good! Forget hair when you have a **HEALTHY GOD**-given life!!! And all the people in the church say, "**AMEN!**"

I love her so much! This is only a **SEASON**.

SUNDAY, AUGUST 13
Rolling Up!

> "Give yourself a few days to be scared. Then roll up your sleeves, get with your physician and beat the heck out of your Cancer."
>
> Melanie Allison Medina,
> ACS Facebook Community Member

THURSDAY, AUGUST 17
Faith (Save the Tatas)

Hi Friends, I'm sure many of you are wondering, "Will she lose her breast?" "Why does she need chemo first?" Or maybe, "Why doesn't she cut them both off?"

Well, let me just say out of all the things that have weighed heavy on me in this journey, it would have to be deciding whether or not to keep my tatas.

I kept wondering to myself, will I make the right decision? What if it comes back? How do I know they'll get all the Cancer if I keep them? And a bunch of other things running through my head.

But thank God for stepping in when I needed Him the most. People would ask me, "What you gonna do? What is it that you wanna do, Evelina?" but I could never honestly give them an answer. But God worked it out in such a way that He's confirmed to me three times, "Honey, I got you!"

CONFIRMATION #1

See…The plan was that if my genetic results came out positive, I would face full reconstruction. Meaning removing both and getting new ones ;) to lower the chances of it coming back if I had the gene, and although that's the route that most people go for peace of mind even without genetic mutation, I still wasn't at peace with that idea. I prayed and I prayed to the point that God answered my prayers, and everything came out **NEGATIVE**. And at one point, my oncologist tried to say, "perhaps it may be an unknown gene" because of my age, and that's when I stopped her and said, "I respect you're the doctor but don't be tryna put any genes on me, the test said no to everything you know to test, and that's just what it is." She was like, "okay," cause seriously unless you can show a positive test result, don't be making stuff up and putting it on me.

CONFIRMATION #2

For my peace of mind, I decided to get a second opinion. **OMG**, have you ever met a doctor who has the ability to give you so much peace? He was amazing and just the right man to confirm to me that he agreed with my chemo plan. He even told me that the chances of it coming back would be very, very low. And that a lumpectomy would be just as effective as complete removal. I'm telling you that man's spirit gave me so much peace that I walked out of there with my head up high, knowing without a doubt that God's got me.

CONFIRMATION #3

Yes...even after that, for some reason, my mind would still entertain the idea of a new breast; but this time, when I arrived at my plastic surgery education appt, for some reason, they were unable to see my online records, and I told her to just cancel it. And it was then I said to myself, "God, I hear ya! I won't even entertain the idea anymore!"

So friends, after three confirmations, I've decided to save the "tatas" and just have a lumpectomy. I just have to trust God that I will have a complete response to chemo so that this mass can shrink small enough to just have that surrounding area removed along with the affected lymph nodes.

Lord, my faith right now is bigger than this Cancer scare. You've told me more than three times it's in your hands, and I've just gotta trust you. Trust you today, tomorrow, and in the days ahead. In Jesus' name, amen!

#walkinginmyhealing

THURSDAY, AUGUST 17
Thank You...

Song of Inspiration:
"Still Say, Thank You" by Smokie Norful

Yes, Lord! I woke up this morning thinking, "Lord, in spite of everything I'm going through, I have to stop and say thank you, Father, because you're showing me that you're with me every step of the way, holding my hand, giving me strength, lifting heavy burdens, Lord you are with me! And I just want to say thank you, Jesus!"

Friends, sometimes we just have to stop and see the blessing in the midst of our storms.

And I have to say Thank You, Jesus, despite this diagnosis…

1. My Genetics came out **NEGATIVE**!!
2. The Cancer is categorized as "good," meaning it usually responds well to treatment.
3. I'm not faced with cutting both breasts.
4. My 4th biopsy spot on the left was just a benign fibroid!
5. My doctors are all so positive.
6. I'm blessed w/ family and friends who love me. (Some people have nobody on this journey to encourage and support them)
7. Free wigs!! Hello!
8. I met a survivor sister who was my food advocate last week (blessing!!)
9. Met another sis...we are both walking this journey together and encouraging one another w/ the word of God
10. I have my sister Tracye in my back pocket
11. My mom and family help us with Emil
12. My heart exam was excellent!
13. So far, I haven't heard anything about my other exams. No news is good news!!
14. I had no immediate reaction to the chemo.
15. I was proactive with my health, and the right Dr. got me into the right program... "Every Woman's Life" for young women under the mammogram age to be

checked for Free!!

16. My port was easily accessed w/ no surgery complications.

17. The doctors see no expiration date on me!!!! (Praise Dance)

18. I will still be able to have children.

19. I'm going to win a contract! (Speaking it!!)

20. I'm alive!!!! Yes!

21. That I know the Lord (without Him, I don't think I'd keep pushing through)

22. Still counting...

So friends, even in the midst of our storms, we must count our blessings. Cause many times when we feel like God has forgotten us and we're all alone, if we would just take the time to be still and list all the positives, we'll realize that He's carrying us every step of the way.

Have a blessed day and Be encouraged

#walkinginmyhealing

FRIDAY, AUGUST 18
The Wrong Chick!

Lord,

You have taught me that faith, as small as a mustard seed, can grow into an amazing tree. Today I ask by faith that you would bring healing from this Cancer. I place my trust in you. May this seed sow healing into every area where the tumor has emerged. May it grow into a strong work, redeeming and restoring with great strength and power.

Amen. (Prayer for the healing of Cancer. | beliefnet.com.)

Thank you for your prayers!!! I honestly don't know how to feel this morning. I'm just putting my trust in the Lord that I'm going to be alright; everything is going to work out, with minimum to no side effects; I'm going to breeze through this. The Lord is going to conquer this, this mass is going to shrink, I'm going to keep my breast, this Cancer is contained, I'm going to impress myself, this mess will never come back, my body will be restored to good health, all in Jesus' precious name. Amen.

Lord, I know you hear my prayers this morning; please dress me with the armor and strength I need to be strong today and every day after. And please ease any worries within me today; your name is the only name powerful enough to do all these things. Hallelujah.

Cancer has messed with the wrong chick! #Healed

FRIDAY, AUGUST 18

Day 1

One down, fifteen more to go. Yeah! As my sister said this morning, "Today marks the day that this journey gets further away in your "rearview mirror."

Well, let me just say the anxiety of not knowing what to expect was what got me. But the overall experience was not bad at all.

My nurse Ashley was an angel; I already love her. She took such good care of me and was patient with her newbie :)

RUN DOWN

When I first arrived, they checked my vitals. I was 100% with my oxygen, I'm not really sure what it means, but hey, that was a great way to start things off.

Afterward, I believe she accessed my port; that's the part I thought was gonna be the scariest, but my sister held my hand, and I did such a good job at numbing it that I didn't even feel it going in. That, to me, was amazing cause that needle was NOT little.

I was then given some premeds and once the blood results came back, I was ready to go!

Receiving the chemo was not bad at all. Praise God, I did not experience any immediate side effects or reactions. Other than my pee was a Lil red for a Lil bit. (Completely normal because the cocktail was red.)

After chemo, I was given a Neulasta shot to boost my white blood cell count. Then a Lupron shot in my booty (ouch!) to protect my ovaries and freeze them because this particular Cancer feeds from my estrogen. Then after four long hours, I was on my way home to relax. (Typically, it'll be three.)

HOW YOU FEELING NOW?

A tiny bit nauseous but overall good; Ashley said I will most likely experience fatigue within a couple days. So I'm taking it easy and relaxing.

Thank you all for your prayers; please know that today's experience was a breeze because you all looked up to the heavens for me. #Healed

SATURDAY, AUGUST 19
Strength

"Strength is looking back and seeing what you have been through and knowing you were strong enough to make it through."

pinkrackproject.com

MONDAY, AUGUST 21
I Give Myself Away

Throughout the many storms in my life, music (gospel in particular) has always served as a source of encouragement for me. Today, "I Give Myself Away" by William McDowell, helps me to remind the Lord that He can use me. Amen.

Be Encouraged.

THURSDAY, AUGUST 24
Just A Chapter

Buenas!

Praise God for waking us up this morning. As for me, I'm grateful to be alive and able to "see" this new day.

Yesterday wasn't easy for me; I woke up with left eye pain. My eye doctor warned me that my eyes may dry out during treatment and that wearing my glasses might be the best thing this season.

But I also think what happened to my eye yesterday was a combination of my sudden sensitivity to the air conditioner, the lil dust particles from the air cabin, or the way I slept the night before.

My sisters took me to the ER cause I could barely open that eye around any light. But the wait was so long (five people in front of me, the first person had already been waiting for three hours). I came home, and my mom gave me an ice pack. So along with prayer, my eye feels so much better this morning. Praise God. I'm just gonna call my Dr around 9 to get a checkup.

I kept reminding myself yesterday, "this is only a chapter in my story" soon, this Cancer will be gone, never to return in Jesus' name! Cause I felt like a mess, looked like a mess, but a lil voice inside of me kept saying, "but Evelina, you are alive! This is not how your story gon' end...fifteen more treatments may seem like a lifetime, but it'll be over before you know it."

So this morning, I'm praising God for my eyesight. Although for a second, I almost panicked when I opened my eyes this morning, and I was like, "**OMG**, I can't see," but it was because I forgot I didn't have my contacts in. Lol.

Other than that, a lil nausea here and there, and my taste buds sometimes disappear. But my mom is definitely making sure I eat.

Thank you all for your continued prayers and support. Xoxoxo

> *"Cancer is only going to be a chapter in your life, not the whole story."*
> — Joe Wasser

FRIDAY, AUGUST 25
Eye Infection

Buenas!

Here's the update:

My eye doctor said I developed an infection in my left eye from my immune system being low.

My bad habit of sleeping in my contacts does not fly this season. Although I shouldn't do it anyway, while on chemo, it's imperative that I don't do it because I'm more prone to infections. So she recommends I keep my glasses handy, especially at night, so my eyes can rest.

Prescription: 7-day steroid drops with follow-up.

Bummer...the reason I barely wear my glasses now is because

I can't even see the big "E" on the eye chart (meaning my prescription is strong); I just know it's there because we all know what an eye chart looks like. (I'm serious!) Smh.

But, thank God I can still "See," and I just gotta do what I gotta do to get better soon.

Thank you all for keeping me prayed up! xoxoxo

> *"I opened two gifts this morning. they were my eyes."*
> livelifehappy.com

SUNDAY, AUGUST 27
Blessed Like That!

Woke up this morning to "Blessed Like That" by Elder Jimmy Hicks And The Voices Of Integrity.

Be Encouraged.

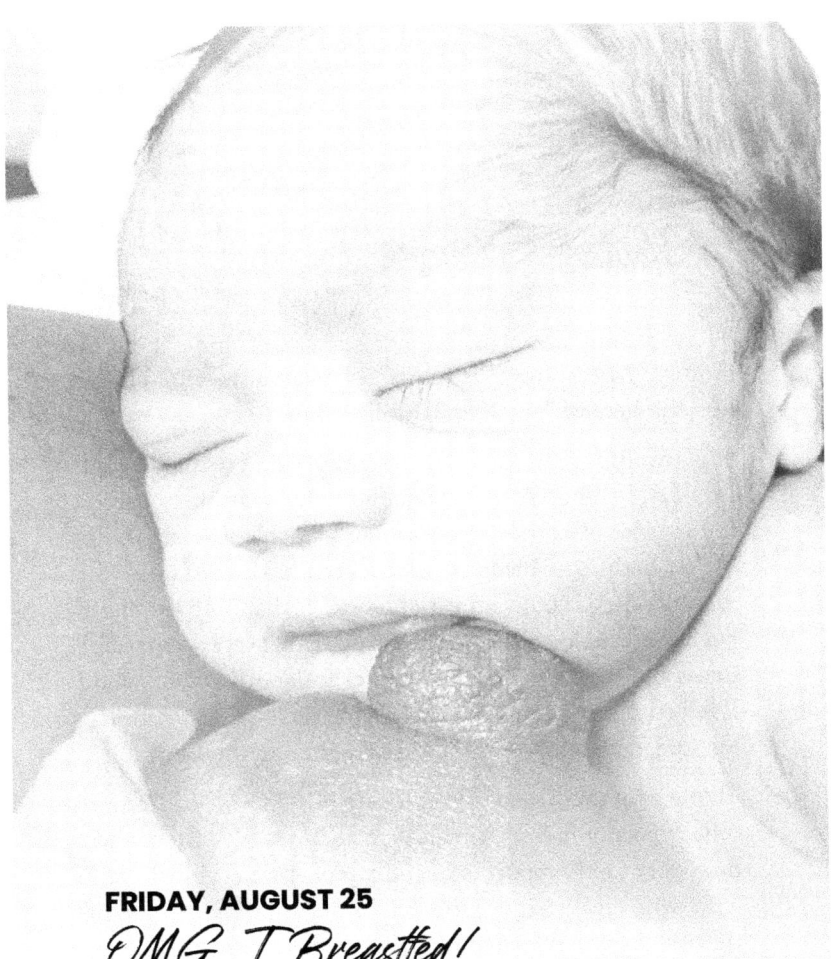

FRIDAY, AUGUST 25
OMG. I Breastfed!

Interesting Fact: "Cancerous cells cannot be passed to your baby through breast milk." - thehealthsite.com/parenting

Therefore even if I did have Breast Cancer at the time I breastfed, baby Emil is safe, and baby #2 will be breastfed as well :)

MONDAY, AUGUST 28
A Mothers Strength

When I think about my father's strength, I think about his mother, "My Granny." A woman of great faith, whom I wish was still here to "pinch up" this little boy. Lol

My grandmother was such a strong woman that, to this very day, I still don't understand how she was able to witness the murder of her youngest son and be able to embrace his lifeless body after being struck by a truck. How?? (smh). But not only did God give my grandmother that kinda strength, but he gave her the strength to then defeat her very own medical issues and to yet again be a caregiver for another dying child. Really, I don't know how my granny did it, but one thing's for sure, her strength was always credited to the Lord.

That's why there's no doubt in my mind that her strength reflects in my father, A man who reminds my sisters and I daily that God's report is the only report we shall believe. A man who enjoys it to the fullest regardless of what life throws his way. A man who's always there to help all others because the lesson is "you never know when you'll need others to help you."

That is the type of role model I desire to be for my son. A mother whom he can reflect on and say, "I know it was her faith that brought her through."

But today, I'm so grateful Emil has no idea what's going on. It makes it easier for me not having to ease his doubts as to whether or not mommy will make it. Or having him see me sick on my worst days. And although many say, "Evelina, but you're being so strong," still for a young child to watch their mother or father go through Cancer is not an easy thing to do. So for his young age, I'm thankful.

But at times, it's just so funny, though, as I see him adapt to the changes... For instance, the first day I cut my hair, he gave me this look that was priceless. It was almost as if he was saying to himself, "Who's that?? She looks like my mommy, but why does she look like that?!? Is that really my mommy?? Wait a minute, something is missing...is that really you, mommy?? "Seriously! He stared at me for so long with this puzzling look on his face. And then, the first day he saw me lay down that wig, he was really even more confused. Lol...He looked at me, then looked at that wig, then he looked at me again and was probably thinking to himself, "well, wait a minute, why is your hair there and you sitting over here?" Lol, Confused as heck! Especially at a time when mommy is teaching you to point to your "HAIR on your HEAD!" lol

But yes, overall, I hope this journey will just be another example of mommies' strength and how God saw fit to use her because He knew that she could be used.

The type of strength that he can reflect on and say, "My mommy is and forever will be among my Heroes."

I Love you, Emil xoxoxo

MONDAY, AUGUST 28
In Jesus Name

"Dear God, May every Cancer cell be wiped out by your powerful hands. Amen!"

EPRAY.COM

TUESDAY, AUGUST 29
Sooo this happened today ...

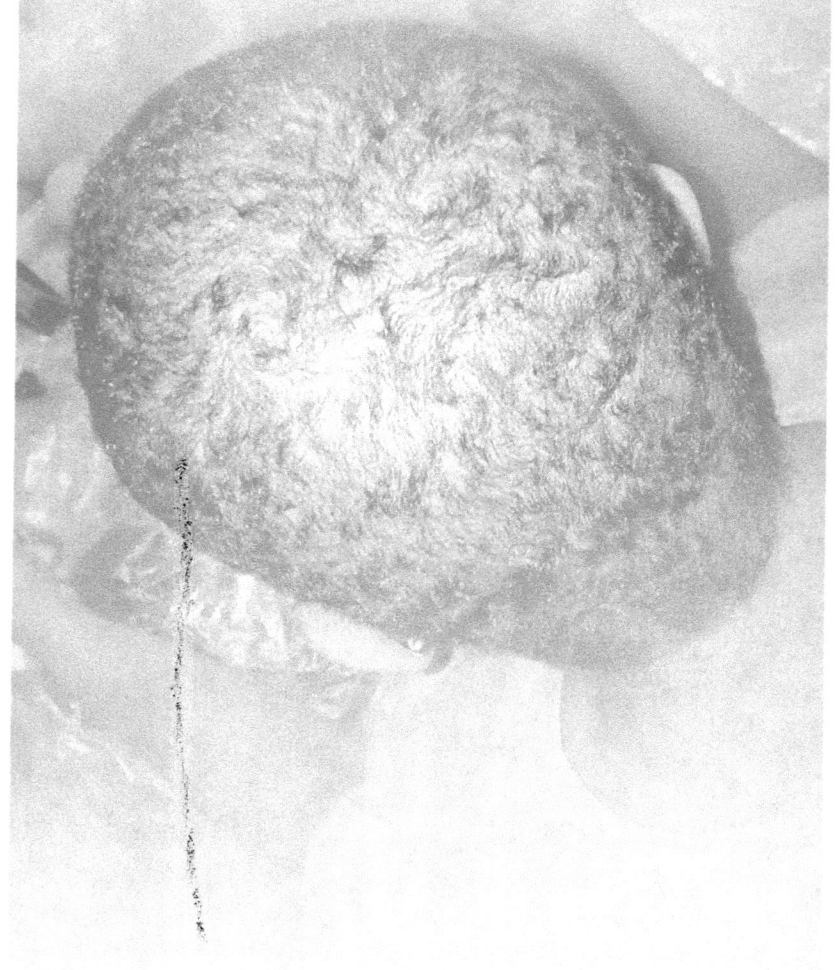

WEDNESDAY, AUGUST 30
The Chop

I knooooow! I made the big chop yesterday. I just couldn't take it anymore. My scalp was irritating me, and after going to the bathroom and noticing other hairs falling off, I said oooooh, nooo! I'm not watching this happen. So I took my baby's clippers and started shaving it off, and the good thing about it is that it didn't matter whether or not I did it right because it's gonna bald anyway. **BTW** Yes! **EVERY** hair on my body will fall off... **EVERY**! Lol, However, they say not everyone loses their eyebrows or lashes.

But yes, my scalp was irritating me because my hair was dying. It no longer curled or anything. It was dry and just a hot mess, so it had to go. But you know what, I never thought I'd be saying this, but I feel so much better like this. Feeling the breeze on my scalp is so soothing, and the overall look is empowering. I just feel like I'm in control...I've got this!

My mom initially wanted to cry because she was in denial that it would fall. But I'm okay with it, really, cause this too shall pass and eventually, she realized that as well and decided to help me finish it off.

So now that I have no hair, my wigs will fit perfectly, and I can wear all the cute little head scarfs. :))

Love you all; your daily encouragement means the world to me.

> *"A woman who cuts her hair is about to change her life."*
> — Coco Chanel

P.S. Emil kept hugging me so much afterward (I wonder if he could sense I needed it)

SATURDAY, SEPTEMBER 2
Round 2

Good moooorning!

Praise God, round two is over.

I meant to post yesterday, but that chemo started taking a toll on me during treatment. So I came home and pretty much rested.

But overall, round two was successful; I'm claiming it's gonna be much better than the first, with no eye infections... #injesusname

My nurse's name was Amanda; she was such a sweetheart. She took excellent care of me, for my usual nurse, Ashley. It's pretty neat how you're assigned the same nurse from start to finish during treatment. Amanda herself mentioned that she loves this particular field because she gets to form a bond w/ her patients, which was an indication to me that she loves what she does. **BTW** they even give me foot massages!

But both ladies are beautiful in spirit, and the overall staff is marvelous. They even had a gentleman that asked me if I wanted to watch movies or listen to music, and I almost took him up on the offer, but y'all know me, I was talking so much in that room that I told him never mind, lol cause it made no sense for me to even look... cause I'm just running my mouth. Lol

Confession

I have to admit I had a little trouble the night before sleeping, just thinking about another treatment. Because you go through the treatments, deal with these crazy side effects, and just when your body is back to normal, it's that time again for another. But that's the life of a chemo patient :/ And I just thank God for getting me through this and for having my family here to help me. They are such a blessing, especially my mom. Without her care, I told the nutritionist I don't know what I would've been eating every day cause I ain't no cook. And before I forget #praisereport, my levels yesterday were all good!! (Sometimes, your blood count and white/red cells go down) So that's credited to my mom cause she has been getting down in the kitchen for me, and my dad has been bringing fresh veggies for my smoothies and meals.

As always, thank you all for your continued prayers and encouraging words; I have a steroid pill (dexamethasone) to take for the next 3 days and the Neulasta that will be injected into me around 4pm.

Love you all xoxoxo

P.S...The center also has a snack basket! Lol

SATURDAY, SEPTEMBER 2

My Morning Inspiration

SUNDAY, SEPTEMBER 3
It's Shrinking!!

Buenas!

I touched my mass for the first time yesterday, and it's shrinking!!!!!!! Hallelujah, Praise God!!!!!

I've been kinda hesitant to touch it, even though I've been told that usually, by the first treatment, chemo starts doing its thing.

I had a large "thick mass," about 5 cm sounds pretty big till you hear about people with 9 cm or more. But still a rather large mass. But anyway, it's blending in and beginning to feel just like the tissue on my left breast.

Omg, I can't believe it!!!

My next oncologist appointment is on the 15th after chemo so she can follow up on how I'm managing with treatment. And to confirm what I'm testifying. How Great is Our God!!!! That's the first song that popped into my mind when thinking of my praise report. The name above all names, worthy of all praise. How great is our God, Hallelujah!!!!

Thank you all for your continued prayers. So far, I'm doing okay with this second treatment. I am about to take my steroids in a few. Love you all so much for everything you do for me. Please know that God is a healer; Cancer is not a death sentence. I do feel bad for those who lose the battle but know that what God has written for someone else, He doesn't have written for you. Their story is their story, and God's testimony for you is totally different. You've got to believe that; I've got to believe that. So I'm walking in my healing cause this is just another bump in the road in my rearview mirror, and I will testify of His Goodness and continue living the good life that He has for me.

God is amazing, He's just using me to help someone through this journey, and I'm okay with that. Even if it changes one person's perspective even if it brings only one person to Him ... I'm okay with that. I'm just honored to be His servant... wish Cancer wouldn't have been the answer, but if that's the way He wants to use me, I'm okay with that because I know He'll bring me through this. And let me add that He'll NEVER EVER bring it back again! (That's my prayer) Hallelujah, Amen!

Have a blessed and wonderful day. XOXOX

Song of Inspiration:
"How Great is our God" by Chris Tomlin

SUNDAY, SEPTEMBER 3

Dream

A few weeks ago, I had a dream. My aunt, who passed away in '02 from Breast Cancer, came to me and said that she wanted me to know that her story would not be my story. #hallelujah

I miss her so much; she's always watched over me. My last memory of her was when I was getting on the greyhound bus with literally no money, and she extended a bag of change towards me and said, "reach in here and take what you can cause you know if I had more, I would give it to you."

#sacrificiallove

RIP Aunt Olivia.

"When passed loved ones appear in your dreams it is often to bring you comfort and support when you need it the most"
@pocketfullofangels, Facebook

MONDAY, SEPTEMBER 4
Glory

> *"And I can't help but give you glory when I think about my story."*
> God Favored Me by Hezekiah Walker

Dear Lord, thank you for this new day and for waking us up this morning. We know that you didn't have to do it. But you did it because you love us unconditionally.

While speaking to my pastor, he asked me, "In this chapter, what is your greatest concern and fear?" I said to him perhaps it would be the unknown of how the side effects will affect me (notice I didn't say dying).

But then again, I said to him, "I believe that whatever aches I may or may not experience, I have to thank God for preparing me. I have been through so much heartache in my life, both physically and emotionally, that I thank God that all of it has prepared me in a way to deal with this. And I believe if I hadn't gone through so much in life, I wouldn't be as mentally stable for what's happening to me now." And he said to me, I agree, and that's an advantage you have in this season.

You see, friends, I would say being hit by that car in '01 is probably the number one reason I keep my head high and trust in the Lord. Many people don't know my testimony, but that night God embraced me in his arms as I spun around multiple times after being hit by a van in ongoing traffic. I literally felt no pain when I landed on the ground. Picture me being 90 pounds if that and my friends and family shaking their heads in disbelief, not knowing how I made it... I remember the paramedics being certain that it had to be more than just a broken pelvis, and I remember the good Samaritan that watched over me till the ambulance arrived, thinking I was crazy when I told him I was eighteen. (He ran and told my mom I was fifteen, lol.) and I remember lying on that stretcher in the ambulance and a paramedic holding my hand, telling me everything was gonna be alright until they told him to move up front and when I reached for the other ones hand, she flat out told me "don't touch me."

Then I remember lying in ICU and my mother seeing me for the first time hysterical with blood all over me and me having the strength to hold her hand to say "everything gon' be alright", not even knowing myself that I was bleeding internally in need of emergency surgery... I then remember waking up too early before the breathing tube was removed and agonizing until they knocked me out again to remove it. I remember the spasms I experienced from my left leg bolted to the bed by screws. And I remember my boss at the time, an excellent makeup artist, telling me that not even all the makeup in the world was going to cover up that scar on my face. I even remember getting home for the first time sitting in that wheelchair crying, reflecting on the experience, thinking about everything the doctors had said about this being a long road to recovery... and perhaps the one thing that gave me the strength to beat the odds was my therapist telling me week after week that there was no way I'd be walking anytime soon.

But what nobody knew was that through it all, I remembered that "God loved me, and He cared, and He would never put more on me than I could bear."

"More Than I Can Bear" by Kirk Franklin

That scar that extended across my face, it disappeared! That statistic of me not walking under their predictions broke the record! Every bone in my body was healed! My son came into this world full-term, healthy, and safe! What the devil meant for evil, God meant for good! It was God who held my hand for the rest of that ambulance ride when that woman told me to let her go. For some reason, God said my child, you shall live tonight and not die, for I have a plan that's greater than you can ever imagine for your life. I'm gonna take you for a ride of your life, and you will be a living testimony for me. You will be used; you will be used!!!

I'm telling you, God is just so amazing. And I just remembered I had a gold chain with the Virgin Mary that popped, and can you believe that chain landed right next to me. That was God telling me, "I'm with you, baby" I know those expensive Jordans don went flying across the road, your cute ponytail has also left the top of your head, lol your purse, which you should've closed before attempting to cross the street has spilled everywhere, but I'm with you, trust me," and that's exactly what I did, I spoke life into my situation, I did not give in to the medical reports, I trusted God and walked in my healing.

And that's why I walk confidently in my healing today. I know He's got me, I know He's healing me, and I know without a shadow of a doubt that I'ma make it through this word "Cancer" that so many of us fear. I know I am because my God said I shall live and not die. I know, I know!!! This is not the end of my story. And just like that car accident, I don't need a settlement from anybody to be a witness for Him. I'm just honored to be used.

But please, Lord, please be gentle on me, don't turn up the fire too high like you did Job, lol there's only, but so much I can take lol. (And for those of you who don't know his story, I advise you to read it. Wanna talk about a man who went through hell and back but still trusted God thru it all...read about Job...awesome story.)

But yes, other than the emotional shock of knowing I have Cancer and the proceeding surgery, I would have to say that being hit by that car is probably the one thing in my life that's prepared me the most emotionally to endure this chapter. It's almost as if some of this doesn't phase me. Most definitely, this is terrible, but I can visualize my healing, so I know God's got this!

Talk about tremendous faith, huh???

But some of you today, just like me, have some even powerful testimonies that you sit back and reflect on and say, "How in the world did I ever make it???! How in the world am I still alive today?!??" Well, I just want you to know right now that God loves you unconditionally, His plan far exceeds our imagination, and just like me, He favors each and every one of you.

Hallelujah! Have a Blessed Day.

Song of Inspiration:
"God Favored Me" by Hezekiah Walker

TUESDAY, SEPTEMBER 5
I'm Not Dying

If you think I'm dying...get out!
If you say I better make it...get out!
God's fighting the battle, I don't want all that pressure,
(I'm doing my best while God does the rest)
If you come at me w/ statistics...get out!
(In the words of my Dr. "Stop the Drama!")
If you think chemo is deadly for me...get out!
(I no guinea pig! I'm a mother with no choice of survival)
If you don't trust God...get out!
(Only faith-filled believers are allowed in my circle.)

I'm sorry, excuse my rant, but God's been too good to me to give up now. In this journey, you wouldn't believe the countless testimonies I've been hearing. There's nothing too hard for my God. Can you believe **HE**…

1. Saved a woman who was given only six weeks to live from Cancer!! 20-something years later, and she is still testifying!!

2. Restored Cancer patients to good health diagnosed w/ lung Cancer!!

3. Healed a woman five years ago from stage 4 kidney Cancer!!

4. Healed a woman 30 something years ago from Breast Cancer!! Then healed her **AGAIN** after reconstructive complications!!

5. Saved a woman from stage 4 metastatic Breast Cancer!!

6. Saved a woman from blood Cancer, who was told the treatments were just too damaging for her to ever have kids, But God!!! She's a mother of two beautiful girls today!!

The testimonies just keep coming and coming!

My point is that there is nothing too hard for God. Many of you, I'm sure, have heard similar testimonies; perhaps you have a testimony of your own. Share it!!! Please!! Someone out there needs to hear it; someone else has just received a diagnosis in which they're thinking, "Lord, this is just too hard for you," "Oh, Lord, my kids!" "Dear God, please don't take me yet!"

It's been said that when the Lord wants to bless you, it usually comes in the form of someone else. Meaning someone today is waiting to hear what you've got to say; someone needs your shoulder to lean on. God did not give that testimony to you for no reason.

Share it!!!! And Bless someone today in the mighty name of Jesus. Cause it's about time to let people know that there is nothing too hard for My God! Amen.

"I am living with (not dying of) Cancer."
IHadCancer.com

Song of Inspiration:
"Can't Give Up Now" by Mary Mary.

WEDNESDAY, SEPTEMBER 6
I Need You Now

Song of Inspiration:
"I Need You Now" by Smokie Norful

This song is exactly what I needed today, for when I'm drained, and out of strength, all I can do is say, "Lord, I need you now."

Be Encouraged.

WEDNESDAY, SEPTEMBER 6
FABYS

Despite how bad that fatigue kicked my butt yesterday, I just had to smile and share my blessing with y'all.

Sooo for those of you that know me very well, y'all know I'm a coupon, thrift store, free clothes, buy one get one free type of girl. Lol...so guess who got a $350 wig for free??? Me!

Heck yeah, I did my research and found a nonprofit online that donates free wigs to Cancer patients. **FABYS**!! All I had to do was email them my diagnosis and my I.D. and choose from the selected styles, and that was it!

Usually, they have the patient try on the wig at a participating salon, but since there's not one in the area, I had to do everything online. In a way, I didn't like it because I thought the wig was a lil darker.. (Y'all know how online shopping can be.) But the overall ordering experience was smooth and easy...so I'm happy! $350, True2life Raquel Welch, lace front, Show Stopper.

Please share the word and be a blessing!!

Thanks, **FABYS**!!! (Fabys.org)

THURSDAY, SEPTEMBER 7
Wow!

Wow! I can only imagine what the back of my head looks like. chemo ain't no joke. **SMH**.

DOES IT HURT WHEN IT COMES OUT??!?

Nah...not at all. I guess the hair follicles just die and uproot themselves from the scalp. (I don't know)

But today, I washed it multiple times, and **VOI-LA**!

Mann... what in the wooorld!!! Go 'head, chemo, do your thang...I ain't mad at ya. Whatever you gotta do to make me betta again.

FRIDAY, SEPTEMBER 8
One Day At A Time

This song has been replaying on my mind aaaalllll day. It took me a while to find the correct version because I haven't heard anyone sing it as beautifully as my aunt.

But today was a tough day for me. The reality of being bald is sinking in.

I never thought that this part of the process would affect me as much as it has... But it's taking an emotional toll on me and I'm soon left to decide if I want to retake control and cut it all off.

I know, I know!! I hear y'all, "it's only hair; it'll grow back, Evelina!"... but still, it was a part of me that I loved.

"Loooord for my sake, teach me to take One Day At a Time."

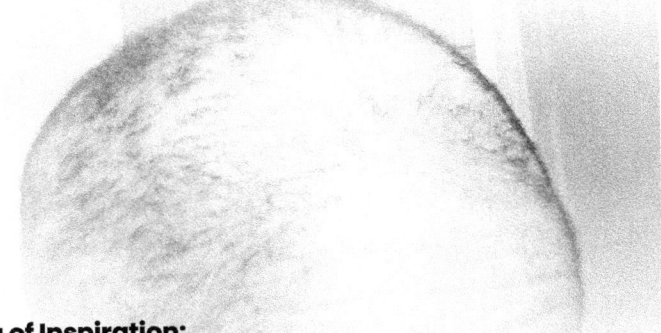

Song of Inspiration:
"One Day At A Time" by Damon Albarn / Robert Delnaja

SATURDAY, SEPTEMBER 9
Oh No!

Good Morniiing!

Praise God for another day...

So guess who gave mommy a cold?!?! Mr. Emil Michelet **WA-TAAAA**!! (I've never seen someone get so excited as he gets about saying his last name, lol.)

Now, my mom is in the kitchen fixing me a nice breakfast, tea, lemon, honey, and all that good stuff cause I have to get rid of this cold **PRONTO**!

SUNDAY, SEPTEMBER 10
No Fear and Uncertainty!

Lately, I've been reflecting a lot on the number one question, "Did they catch it on time?" and I've been thinking about how my response so far has been "well, I don't know my stage," "I believe so," or I'll refer back to when "I think" it all started."

Ookaaay, so what's the problem here?!?! Why the heck am I talking with fear and uncertainty at times?!?!" No-no-no, Evelina, you know so! You've got to speak life and speak it confidently cause you ain't going nowhere. You are here to stay and live the rest of this beautiful life God has planned for you. What the heck do you mean?? "I guess so??" get it together, girl!

Y'all excuse me while I get myself in check. Lol, sometimes you've just got to "Encourage Yourself" cause if you don't, no one else will.

Of course, they've caught it early! I've got to believe that and speak it with confidence. My surgeon said he sees no expiration date on me! My scans all came out great. Otherwise, treatment would've been interrupted (I would think), and my diagnostic Dr. said according to what he saw, he felt it was early (he does this every day).

Maaann if I was going anywhere, they would've called me in by now and said, "Ms. Johnson, there's no need to even do chemo." So yes, I'm tripping and I need to get it together and speak the truth.

Now ask me again, "Did they catch it on time??"...Cause "Yes, praise God!" Is what my answer will be!

Song of Inspiration: "Encourage Yourself" By Donald Lawrence

SUNDAY, SEPTEMBER 10

Pink Power <3

"Breast Cancer sucks, but when you have family and friends for support, it makes it bearable."
Alisha Ann Pelt

MONDAY, SEPTEMBER 11
Bald and Beautiful

TUESDAY, SEPTEMBER 12
Look Good Feel Better

I just wanted to share with y'all my testimony from a **FREE** class I took called Look Good Feel Better. A program designed for women undergoing treatment that not only teaches us about skincare, makeup and head wraps but also self-esteem so that we're not walking around looking like what we are going through.

It was amazing and absolutely beneficial in helping me embrace my baldness.

Oh yeah, and guess what?????

Each participant receives a FREE COSMETIC KIT worth over $300!!!

So y'all know I'm happy, lol.

I got free maaaakeup... I got free maaaakeup... I got free maaaakeup... lol.

Share the Blessing!

For more information, visit lookgoodfeelbetter.org.

WEDNESDAY, SEPTEMBER 13
"THE" Doctor

Buenassss!!

Hope everyone is off to a great start... This morning I'm traveling to Franklin, VA, for work. I haven't been in about two/three weeks due to treatment and side effects, but thank God for allowing me to go this morning and make it to church Sunday.

I'm still dealing with this cold, but I said to myself, "I don't care, I haven't been to church in a while, and I haven't been to work...I'm going!" Especially because I'll be back to glasses Friday, and when I wear my glasses, I can't really drive long distances.

But anyways, the Lord is good! All the time!!

Yesterday I had an amazing experience with my primary care physician. I made an appointment to see him, so I could catch him up on some things, and can y'all believe this man asked me if I was in remission?!?? It's funny cause he said he's been getting all the faxes from the diagnosis, but when he saw me yesterday, he was confused. He kept thinking the paperwork was from 2016, although he's getting everything as I'm going through the treatments. I said to him, "Remission?!?? I'm telling you I'm going through treatments now!" And he said, "You don't look like it!" ...Amen to that!!! Then he said something I had never heard a doctor say before. He said, "Before you leave, I wanna pray with you" in my mind, I was thinking, "wow!!!". I rave about my surgeon and all the positive things he says to me about God, but I have NEVER had a Dr. Pray with me.

I wish many more would because he knows who's really **THE DOCTOR**. Yeah, Doctors have the degree and education, but ultimately God has the final say.

My physician just wanted to pray that I continue being positive, speak healing over me, and assure me that he's on #TeamEvelina.

Praise God for him... it was beautiful... it was amazing... I declare a blessing over his practice.

Amen.

THURSDAY, SEPTEMBER 14

100!

"Shrink Tumor, Shrink!"

Declaration:
My chemo is working! My tumor is shrinking! My body is responding 100% to treatment! Every Cancer Cell is gone! and I'm walking in my healing, in the name of Jesus... Hallelujah!

Please keep me in prayer tomorrow; not only do I have treatment, but I will see my oncologist for the first time to confirm the shrinkage. I'm sooo excited to receive the good news. In the name of Jesus, I declare that I am Cancer free! Amen.

FRIDAY, SEPTEMBER 15

#Winning!

Yaaay!!! The power of spoken words is real, I'm telling you. God is soooo amazing... I gotta say it again. He's sooo amaaaaazing!!! Woooo!

It's absolutely shrinking....my doctor is just so amazed by my body's response to treatment and my overall appearance. She said I'm the new face of a "Cancer patient" because most of us think a patient looks broken down and ready for the grave... but "my story" brings back hope because Cancer is definitely not a death sentence.

OMG, I'm sooo excited! God is so good; she said the tumor is significantly shrinking to the point that she could barely find it. It was initially 5 cm and today it's 2.5 - 3 cm and still shrinking in the name of Jesus!!!

I declare... I'm Cancer-free!!! I'm Cancer-free!!!

Praise God; I'm a winner! #Healed!

SATURDAY, SEPTEMBER 16
80%

Yesterday my oncologist said **80% of my healing was attributed to God and my support system.**

And I want to take this time to thank you All for all your encouraging words and prayers and for just following my blog. Your support means the world to me. I told Dr "K," I don't know how I would've made it without such a strong prayer circle. Isn't God amazing?? I hope my journey continues to inspire you as you inspire me.

Keep on trusting God, warriors; there is absolutely nothing too hard for Him. He can move **ANY** mountain, cure any disease and even raise the dead. He's simply that amazing.

It's sooo sad, as my Doctor said, not everyone has someone to hold their hand during treatment, at home, or even anytime throughout their journey. I am blessed! And I want to thank you all sincerely from the bottom of my heart. #grateful.

SATURDAY, SEPTEMBER 16
He Has His Hands On "ME"

Song of Inspiration:
"He Has His Hands On You" by Stan Jones

What a beautiful reminder that God will **ALWAYS** have His hands on me. **NO MATTER WHAT.**

Amen. Be Encouraged.

MONDAY, SEPTEMBER 18
Warrior Cry

Buenas!!

Waking up this morning with this Lil boy stuck to me; I swear lately it seems like he can't sleep in his bed; he just gotta be stuck right on momma for a good night's sleep. Smh, lol.

Great news, my cold is gone' yeah!!! I feel so much better, and so far, this treatment is going well. One more strong treatment on the 29th, then I'll start a new med for twelve weeks called Taxol to finish chemotherapy! I'm sooo ready to bang that bell that I know the entire building gon' hear me when I'm done. No joke! Everybody gon' know I've got the victory!... Yes! Yes! Yes! I can't wait.

Well, this morning, I wanna talk about the "Warrior Cry." Just a week ago, I heard a radio host say, "Every soldier needs a warrior cry," and when she said that, it took me back to the first day I met my oncologist. I was so distraught; the news was still fresh to me, and although I knew God was my healer, just the thought of what was to come as far as treatment was tearing me up. I think that was probably the first time I ever cried tremendously over my health. In my other two experiences, I teared up a bit, but this time my oncologist embraced me, and so did my sister cause it was too much info for me to handle. Then hearing what people would say to me about chemo doing this and that to you weighed on me. I said to her in my cry, "Thank God my baby doesn't have to watch me suffer," "I don't wanna be here," "I told them something wasn't right," and some other things I can't remember. But like my doctor said to me the next time she saw me, "You needed to cry, you needed to release it" and she's right because we often try so hard to be strong for our family and everyone looking from the outside while we're silently tearing up on the inside, but at times we need to release that battle cry...let it out...talk to God...then get back up and keep it moving ...knowing that God has heard you and He'll never leave you nor forsake you.

So this past Friday, when some of the nurses saw me for the first time, they were so happy. They remembered seeing me crying broke down in the lobby that day, but now ...Look at God! He rose me back up and gave me the strength I needed to face this diagnosis like the warrior He created me to be.

Everyone is just so amazed it's even the same "ME" I no longer look the same nor am I breaking down at the thought of knowing it's Cancer. I'm just confidently walking in my healing, looking good, feeling better thanks to ACS, rocking my wig thanks to FABYS, and claiming that I am Cancer free cause I'm ready for the next phase in my life. I keep telling the center I'ma be working with them, bringing awareness with my gift one way or another. It's always been a dream of mine, so we'll see what connections I make... but life is sooo good, I'ma make it. I had my warrior cry; now it's time to rejoice because the Lord has promised me that He will never leave me nor forsake me.

So friends, keep your head up high, have your warrior cry but don't stay down, knowing that God is able to do all things exceedingly, abundantly, above and beyond what we think He's capable of doing for us. He's a good God; take a look at my story, for example; He's simply amazing!

Hallelujah!

"A Warrior will cry in her circumstance but wipe her tears away and get back up. She is not a slave to bad news because she knows who her Lord is and that He will fulfill His promises."

truebeautyministries.com

MONDAY, SEPTEMBER 18

Joy.

WEDNESDAY, SEPTEMBER 20
Pep Talk

"Dear Me. You are awesome, strong, marvelous, loved, smart and special! I just thought I would remind you. - Love Me"

RAMANAN

THURSDAY, SEPTEMBER 21
I Can Do This!

Hi Everyone!

Sorry I haven't posted like I regularly do. But my tummy is so much better now, and whoever suggested apple juice knows what they talkin bout :)) Let me tell ya, it worked waaayyy better than them meds. So that'll be my #1 go-to from now on. Lol.

Soo...After the constipation issue followed the fatigue...the anxiety...and this morning, I noticed my tongue getting black spots. Ahh maaan another darn side effect.

But the bright side is I'm alive and getting treated. Right?!

Cause just this week, I heard a testimony about a lady who could not get chemo because it was paralyzing her body. Wow! Therefore, the doctors just removed her mass, and she prayed for God's healing. And in time, that's just what He did! Amazing, isn't it??

Therefore I can't complain, and I gotta keep asking God for the strength I need each day when I'm down. Cause there are days, I tell ya, I just wanna explode... Especially now, since I'm temporarily menopausal and Emil has his breakdowns, I feel fatigued, and then the Libra in me kicks in....it gets crazy. (oh yeah and on top of that, I'm a short Latina! Lord have mercy) lol

Yep, those days I do my hardest to remind myself, "Evelina, you are stronger than this, Evelina, you can make it. Evelina, thirteen more to go, Evelina, it'll never return again. Evelina, you are alive. Evelina, this is only a test, Evelina. Thank God for a cure, Evelina; you are Healed!" Self-encouragement…I just got to do it.

TUESDAY, SEPTEMBER 26
It's A New Season!

Song of Inspiration: "It's A New Season" by Israel Houghton / Derick Wayne Thomas

Yes! What a beautiful reminder that soon I'll be entering into a **NEW SEASON**.

Amen

THURSDAY, SEPTEMBER 28
Grateful

Hiiii everyone.

Tomorrow is my last dose of AC (strong treatment). Yaaay!!! I told my massage therapist, "I wanna bang that gong!!" Because I'm getting so close to this being all behind me. Yes!

Today I had a full-body clinical massage courtesy of the center. Sorry I was chatting so much that I didn't take a selfie, but I'll get her on camera tomorrow. :) It was so relaxing and much-needed to de-stress my feelings so far.

Then that afternoon, I just had to thank the man that God used to save my life, Dr. "N." He was the one who, without hesitation, connected me to the Every Woman's Life Program. Without his quick action, I would probably still be worried about my breast concern. He's awesome, and I praise God for him every day.

Speaking of him, the entire team at Riverside has been superb. From diagnostics on down...I love my new family! For they promised me that they would walk with me every step of the way if I proceeded, and without a doubt, they've done just that!

God Bless them!

BTW Dr. "N," asked me, "Are you doing chemo"? ...lol. Yes, Dr.! I'm the new face of treatment :)

THURSDAY, SEPTEMBER 28
15!

FYI...

The reason why everyone reacts differently to Breast Cancer

is not only because of their genetic makeup but because there are fifteen different types of Breast Cancers, in addition to the hormone receptors of their particular kind.

The kind I have is **IDC**, Invasive Ductal Carcinoma **ER/PR + HeR2** - Stage: #Healed

No two Cancers are ever the same.

So there you have it! **#BEINFORMED**.

FRIDAY, SEPTEMBER 29
Victory!

Yaay!! Today was the last day of my first chemo regimen, AC (Adriamycin and Cytoxan). And, you darn right, I banged that gong!! Four times to be exact :) That even the office and a gentleman walking up the steps heard me. Lol.

Now I'm moving on to Taxol with only twelve treatments left. Whoopee!

Praise God that chapter of my life is over. He's a healer for sure, and to be honest, after every treatment, there was Victory! Cause I got closer and closer each week to being Cancer-free. Lord, you are sooo good (I love you for healing my body). Again today, I also got a foot massage :)

I must admit I felt drained by this treatment for some reason; I just had many things on my mind. But I made it through with a smile, especially because that was my last AC.

Well, that's all, folks :))) thank you for praying for me. I've got the Victory! Because the devil was defeated, and God is to be Praised. Hallelujah!

Song of Inspiration: Victory by Tye Tribbett and G.A.

SUNDAY, OCTOBER 1
Riverside Diagnostic

Today I want to thank Dr. "P." For I'll never forget me telling him, "I have no choice," and he said to me, "You do have a choice cause many choose not to follow through," and I said to him, "well I don't have a choice, I have to do what you tell me to do."

Yes, hearing him say, "Okay, we have to talk," after he saw my scans was hard. Yes, it was tearful going through the biopsy. Yes, it was heartbreaking to see the "iceberg" in his eyes (like

Rose said in Titanic) before knowing the final results. But through it all, it was comforting to know I had a savior by my side, blessing the hands of every Dr. and nurse who took care of me. Even on July 11, when they broke it down, they said, "I can't promise you it'll be easy, but I can tell you that you will make it!"

Then, on that day, they blessed me with my amazing navigator, Elizabeth, who is like a guidance counselor. She's fantastic, for she took care of my insurance right away, connected me to the best surgeon, told me all about the Cancer center, listened to my cry, broke the news to my sister, and informed me more about my diagnosis ... what a blessing she's been.

God Bless them all.

> *"I became a doctor because I wanted to help women."*
> Dr. P.

TUESDAY, OCTOBER 3
Taxol

Lately, I've been thinking a lot about my upcoming weekly treatments. Having to go from every two weeks to weekly has me nervous. It already takes me a week to bounce back; I can't imagine the weekly effect. But to God be the glory, cause I know Ima make it regardless. I must admit it's just tiring at times; even right now, I'm still fatigued. But I managed to be productive with my t-shirt campaign today.

Thank you all for your prayers. Dec 29th, I believe, is my final chemo!!!

Nearing the finish line!

FRIDAY, OCTOBER 6

Cancer! Last night I couldn't help but to just think about this darn Cancer. Like, how in the world did you just invade my body? How can you just come into my system and change my whole world? I had plans next weekend; I had plans this year, like how can you just flip my life this way???

But besides the bad, you have opened my eyes to what truly matters. My son...

Although I don't consider myself to be doing the best I can for him, he protects me every night. He comforts me by wrapping his arms around me and crawling all over me as if he is still in my womb, looking for that comfortable spot up against me.

My Support System...

You have surrounded me with people who give me words of encouragement, a helping hand and rooting for me to the finish line.

My Healthcare...

Although this sounds crazy, you came at perfect timing. Thank God for the funding that supports the Every Woman's Life Program and the specialized Breast Cancer insurance... Thank God for the Center itself! These Drs. have given me so much hope for a brighter future.

Life...

You've made me realize that my life can be flipped upside down within seconds. Who would've thought I'd be healthy one second and diagnosed the next.

My Family...

I can't even express it enough; everyone has cared for me like they always do.

Cancer...I don't know how you did it, but my journey with you has been bittersweet.

FRIDAY, OCTOBER 6

My Stall

"Sometimes God holds you back temporarily until the road is safe and clear to continue. Be thankful for the stall."
unknown

FRIDAY, OCTOBER 6

STILL

Amid this battle, I've found myself becoming very distant from life.

Perhaps it's because I feel the calling to be **STILL** in this season.

You see, chemo be wearing me out for a couple of days, then I try my best to catch up with work, and on top of that, God's been shifting another area in my life right in the midst of this storm. So I'm just like, "Lord! I hear you! This season it's exclusively just you and me."

Then I hear Him saying..."I need your undivided attention."

Yes, I'm still positive, motivated, and happy to be healed, but the reality is dealing with Cancer is life-changing. Even right now, as I'm writing this, I'm thinking, "Man, I'm Hot!" As a result of the menopause side effects… then every other day, as pretty as that wig is, I think, "I want this wig off!" because it is so freaking hot outside. Then having to switch up corrective lenses between treatments… being careful of this port within me at night. I get so tired!

Again...But God!

So I apologize to anyone if I seem distant at the moment. Please continue praying for my strength and healing. And know that this is only just a season for me to be **STILL**.

Love you all. <3

"The quieter you become, the more you can hear."
Ram Dass

SUNDAY, OCTOBER 8

Chemo?!?

"You're a Mother! You have no choice."
Dr. K.

Yesterday, while talking to my sis, I mentioned to her how people often say chemo is not good for you. And she said to me, "Have those people gone through Cancer?"

And she's right; it's easy to say what you would and wouldn't do when you're on the sidelines. I honestly had no other choice as far as my treatment, and even if I did, I bet you $100 I would still be at home contemplating what to do...as indecisive as I am.

My advice is, please don't tell a Cancer patient their treatment is unsuitable. We already have a lot on our minds, and if we choose chemo, we're choosing what we feel is the most effective method for us.

Yes, there will be some side effects and maybe even pain, but that's nothing compared to dying. Besides, Cancer does not look the same for everyone... Do I look like I'm about to pass out? Am I in a wheelchair? Am I in a walker? Nooo! Am I knocking on death's door?? No!

It is what it is; yes, I lost all my hair, but it'll grow back and be long and pretty again. I just had to do whatever it took to save my life and live for Emil.

So please don't let your idea of what you've seen some patients go through make you think chemo is deadly. Cause chemo right now is helping me kick this Cancer's butt!

#SURVIVOR #4BABYEMIL

MONDAY, OCTOBER 9

Lina Imaging

As many of you know, I'm the owner of LinaImaging.

But ever since chemo, I've found it a Lil hard to keep up with my work. Even right now, I'm thinking about a project that I haven't been able to get to for months due to extreme fatigue and contract responsibilities. Even with the contracts, I have to take it easy at times.

It's crazy cause I was telling my first lady, "I ain't think it was gon' be like "**THIS!**"

Meaning: I never thought anything would take me away from my graphics. 4 Real! I lived and breathed on that computer. It was my world! In fact, just at the beginning of this year, I had a system crash, and I cried like a baby. It truly broke my heart!

I'm so addicted to my work. I love my clients; I love their visions; I love what I do; I just love the gift God has blessed me with.

It's incredible how chemo just changed all that temporarily. Yes! Temporarily cause I'll be rocking it again once all this is over.

But on the upside, guess what? If it weren't for this season, I probably would've never truly pursued my writing.

Blogging has been sooo therapeutic for me. It's my comfort, my release, my way of talking to God late in the midnight hours. And Because of You and the tremendous encouragement from my leaders, I can say I have another **VISION** coming true…

A book: "#Healed: A Diary From Cancer to Surviva"

#PUBLISHEDAUTHOR **#**COMINGSOON

MONDAY, OCTOBER 9
Say What!

Yes! Tonight I'm thrilled to say...

My Lump Shrunk!

THURSDAY, OCTOBER 12
The News...

Telling your friends that you have Cancer can be a hard thing to do. Especially cause everyone's faith level is different, and you must be extremely careful as a Cancer patient who you allow into your journey.

Only Positivity Allowed

I'm so grateful for each and everyone one of you. When talking to my cousin the other day, I realized I currently have 65 followers, and out of the 65, maybe four or five are actual family members. (Wow! I know...I said the same thing, but that's another story lol) But you wanna know something incredible?!? I haven't done the calculation, but many of you are new friends God has placed in my life to encourage me in this journey. Thank you! Thank you! It means the world to me that more and more people are rooting me to the finish line.

Again if you or someone you know is battling Cancer and don't know how to break the news to a friend, here's a recollection of my email.

"Hi _____, I wanted to share something with you, my prayer warrior. And before I do, all I want is positive thinking because that's all I need in order to get through this new season God has for me.

I went for the mammo, and my right breast is positive. Tuesday, I got the news. Wednesday, I saw the surgeon, but on the 25th, I see my oncologist.

Feelings are all up in the air. I've asked God, "why me? I've been through so many drastic things with my health," and He's responded, "why not you, Evelina? You are strong. You are a survivor. You look up to me, and I know that when I heal you, you will testify my goodness and help many others... I can count on you, my daughter."

So I have to trust God; despite the treatments and the surgeries, I have to trust Him, and as I write this, I know He's already healing me. I don't know the stage, and honestly, I don't wanna know because I don't want it to be a stumbling block in my mind. I have to guard all my thoughts and have only people around me that know that God is a healer. I've been declaring this week, "I am healed and I made it!" I know for a fact that there is power in spoken words. I walked! Sooner than they expected, I made it despite the negative comments of my therapist. God woke me up in that hotel room all alone after passing out; the doctors couldn't explain how I was living with so much blood backed up in me, but thank God for the donor whose blood runs through me for saving my life. I made it then, and I'll make it through this.

We all know it won't be easy, but I'm going to make it. My surgeon says he has faith in me and needs me to be strong and think about my life because he sees no expiration date on me. So when I'm down, I just need the people around me to remind me at all times that I will make it, that God has a purpose for me and that I need to be strong if I ever feel like giving up.

I have my son, my family, and a great support system. Therefore I know I can trust you to encourage me because you are a woman/man of God.

I'll keep you updated; I have to see the oncologist on the 25th to see what my treatment plan will be, but my surgeon is thinking most likely chemo and radiation. But they have to be on the same page as far as how they wanna do the surgery and treatment. Right now, they're tryna have an idea of how I developed Cancer at my age.

My surgeon wants to consider removing that breast and then the reconstruction. Or removing both...he said he can't make me, but it's something I have to consider. The insurance will cover the reconstruction when the time is right.

Please don't say, "I'm sorry to hear this...simply say you'll be praying for me at all times and that you know I'll make it" cause I will!!

Cancer is not a death sentence, but I'm not sharing this with the world. Cause to be honest, not everyone wants your healing and what's best for you.

Love, Evelina.

THURSDAY, OCTOBER 12
Prayers

Please keep me in your prayers for tomorrow. As usual, I'm nervous about treatment.

"YOU NERVOUS, EVELINA?!?"

Yes, I know I speak positivity and all, but every time that needle connects with my port, I get nervous.

This time it's because it's a new medication with perhaps new side effects. I did extremely well with AC which is a very strong treatment, and I pray I do even better with Taxol. In fact, some people have to take additional chemos sometimes with Taxol due to their pathology report. So I'm grateful it's just one med for me.

But oh mann, smh...

I have to take my meds differently starting tonight. Five pills at 10 pm, five pills at 4 am! Versus two pills twice daily for three days starting the day after treatment. Then Benadryl during every single treatment. I'm feeling overwhelmed tonight.

Cause Taxol is a chemo where they really take a lot of preventative actions because some patients demonstrate an allergic reaction to it. But we're claiming I'm not!

But yes, friends, Taxol is it! My last chemo regimen to the finish line. May every Cancer cell be cast out in the name of Jesus.

Keep me in your prayers for little to no side effects. Thank you all. Love, Lina.

> *"Heavenly Father, may every Cancerous cell be cast out and replaced with a good one. May every spot of this deadly cell be wiped out by your powerful hands. Amen"*
> ePray.com

FRIDAY, OCTOBER 13
Taxol Day 1

Hi everyone!

Day one of Taxol went really good; thank you for your prayers. No immediate reaction! Just drowsy from Benadryl today, and that's to be expected. So I slept for about five hours when I got home.

Today I also saw my oncologist; she was so happy to wear my shirt. And it worked out perfectly cause today was Breast Cancer shirt day. It just happened that no one told her, so when I gave her the shirt, she immediately changed into it. Lol

What else happened...hmm.

My greedy butt sister Tanya came to my appointment today. Took about ten snacks from the goodie bag. Lord have mercy... **SMH** as if she hadn't eaten all day. Lol, had the nurses up in there talking bout us. It runs in the family cause I be grubbing. Someone special in my life reminds me about my eating habits allll the time. Lol, but it's alright. I will definitely replace some things in the basket by the next visit.

Oh yeah, my highlight of the day was that my tumor is disappearing for sure. Woot! Woot! My doctor believes it's just breast tissue that she's feeling now!! Amen! I'm so happy; she's happy...my body responded 100% to chemo, and I can't wait for the scans to confirm. Thank you all for your continued prayers.

P.S. Lol, another wig compliment. A lady from the center asked me how long I'd been on chemo cause she was impressed that my hair hadn't fallen yet. She and the front desk lady said they loved it! Thanks again Faby!!!

FRIDAY, OCTOBER 13
Inspire

> "I want to inspire people. I want someone to look at me and say "because of you, I didn't give up."

UNKNOWN

SUNDAY, OCTOBER 15
Making Strides

We're back at it again! This time, it's even more personal...

Special thanks to everyone who came out and supported us and those who were there in spirit.

It was an awesome event, and I am so blessed to be among the countless survivors.

God's a Healer! Thank you, Team #Healed.

We made it!!!

MONDAY, OCTOBER 16
I Love You Tanya

My sister's post really moved me yesterday.

Words cannot express how blessed I am to have them.

> Feeling blessed this Sunday to be doing this walk for my sister ♡ I can't imagine what you are going through during this time..but what I do know is that I am here for you 1000000000% hands down....you are not alone ..quite often when we hear about these tragedies we just say sorry to hear that and then continue with our daily routines in life..but when it hits so close to home you have a whole different perspective and outlook on life...especially once you start going to treatments with the individual.as I sat in there I cried as I watched them stick my sister..and she looked at me and said it don't hurt ...I am honored to be here today with my family and new found friends.... I pray for all affected by this terrible disease... I am here for the long run for my sister. ..you are and will be a survivor...you can count on me TODAY TOMORROW AND FOREVER!!!!! I LOVE YOU Evelina Johnson Buendia♡♡♡ this too shall pass!!!!

WEDNESDAY, OCTOBER 18
It Aches

Hi friends!

So far, this treatment has been better than the A/C. I am experiencing some aches, but I'm not sure if it's due to Sunday's event or just a side effect. But the next treatment will tell for sure.

Yesterday while speaking to my friend, I told her, "I hope I'm not making anyone think this is easy, but rather inspire them to keep a positive attitude if they ever face such a situation" cause this is not easy.

This season has really taught me to reanalyze some things in my life and to prioritize what's really important, "**ME**"! The one person I've pushed to the side for so long. Even my supervisor had to remind me initially, "Evelina, we need you to focus on your healing first!" Although one would think that should be a no-brainer, I needed to hear that. I needed to hear that word from God. Cause being self-employed is not easy, and all sorts of thoughts run through your mind, especially when you can't work for days. But thank God! Cause **HE** always provides, cause that's just the kinda God He is.

Have a blessed day.

Love, Lina.

FRIDAY, OCTOBER 20
Attitude

Yessss, I know I should be asleep, but I just finished a project, and on top of that, at 4 am, I have to take my meds. Ughhhh, this 4 am regimen is driving me crazy. But anyways...

Today my maintenance man told me, "You have just about the best attitude I've ever seen; I don't think I could do it."

It's because I'm **HEALED**, sir! I know for sure I ain't going nowhere. But even if I was, I would have to say I don't think I'd be so sad either. Because where I'd be going would be a much better place than here. That's for sure!

I also can rest assured that my son would be taken care of, that I'd have many pastors to speak about me and not just be reading a bio from a piece of paper, and thanks to life insurance, I know I would not be leaving a burden on my family.

Yes, I said it, and I know, I know, I shouldn't be speaking about death, but I'm just keeping it real. Cause with God, there's nothing to fear.

But he's right; I give myself a pat on the back because I sometimes skim through my pictures and say to myself, "I don't know how I do it."

All I know is that my hallelujah belongs to you, Lord! I knew there was no way you would've brought me this far to end it all now.

You've purposed me for something far greater than I can imagine. You have plans to fulfill all my dreams and to make my cup overflow. Lord, you are mighty, and I know that in this season, you'll reveal to me something magnificent. You deserve Praise for my attitude, and I'm glad that I'm shining because of you. Please uphold me until the end of this journey so that I may be able to inspire many others.

In Jesus's name. Amen.

> *"I am too positive to be doubtful, too optimistic to be fearful, and too determined to be defeated."*
> — unknown

FRIDAY, OCTOBER 20
My Hallelujah

Song of Inspiration: "You Deserve It" by James Hairston / Phontae Reed / Cortez Vaughn / David Bloom

Lord, my Hallelujah belongs to you and only you!

FRIDAY, OCTOBER 20

Taxol Day 2

Today was a pretty good day; my Lil sis Heike came to treatment with me. She even helped me make a vlog today.

Due to the Benadryl I have to take now, I'm actually pretty drowsy during and after treatment. Even before chemo Benadryl would knock me out, so having to take 2 pills now; Mann, I be sooo sleepy when I get home.

As usual, my visit to the center was pretty good.

I brought them some gifts, such as snacks, books, and a bear that sings "I Hope You Dance," which was given to me by my former coworkers. She really cheered me up during my stay at the hospital and over the years, so I wanted to bring some sunshine to the center. They loved it so much they are gonna keep it at the receptionist's desk to play with her every now and then. So happy they loved it. If she's still there next Friday, I'll take a pic of her.

Another gift I brought to the center was my testimony. I shared with a couple of nurses today why I smile in the midst of my storm. One of them said to me, "God is so great you may not even need surgery other than port removal" She was very inspired. Another one said you are a "bionic woman." But I say it is God's strength that holds me up. Like I told my friend, I'm so happy I had Emil when I did cause late at night, when I feel emotional, he somehow knows how to hug me and to remind me to keep it together.

Overall today's visit was good; ten more; thank you, Jesus! I have a feeling tomorrow holds a special surprise for me. Keep me in prayer for a wonderful response to Taxol. He can do it!

Love, Lina

MONDAY, OCTOBER 23
Tingling

Hi everyone!

Thank you for your prayers; I'm still doing good; in fact, I was on the computer earlier, motivating myself to do some work while I had the energy.

Man, last night, it felt like my whole body was tingling; the sensation had started earlier that day and gradually seemed to increase. But thank God this morning it went away, but I definitely gotta let my doctor know if it persists because Taxol can cause nerve damage that, if not treated right away, can be irreversible, they say. But that won't be me!

Today I also had a wonderful time at one of my support groups. It's funny cause I really wasn't fond of this group from the beginning because I felt like I needed to be surrounded more by believers, especially in the beginning when I was all to pieces. But tonight was different, and after two months of skipping out, I am strong enough not to really need that sort of support from them but to be able to fellowship with other women and inspire them with my testimony.

As a matter of fact, after tonight, I am definitely publishing my journey. There are so many women who are distraught and broken...there are so many without a strong support system, and there are so many who need to be encouraged by the word of God from someone who has been there.

Dear Lord...I aspire to inspire.

THURSDAY, OCTOBER 26
Covered

Last week while speaking to My Pastors, I said to them, "Sometimes I pretend I don't even have Cancer!".

Now some of you may be saying, "Girl, this ain't nothing to be playing with!"

But seriously, I believe not dwelling on the disease and living my life as normally as possible has really contributed to my healing. To the point that even the people around me are starting to forget.

For instance, this morning, I was sharing with Mrs. Kathy about a conversation I had with one of my coworkers. And how she accidentally made a remark about feeling bad at the thought that Cancer sadly reoccurs in some patients.

Now, although I knew she really didn't mean no harm in saying it, nor would she dare say anything to hurt my feelings. It did kinda bother me a tiny bit because the reality of it is I'm still a Cancer patient. And she totally forgot.

So that night, as I was giving my cousin an update on my health, I mentioned the incident to her, and she then said to me. "Your friend is a testimony that you are Cancer-free! Look at how she has forgotten about the disease, that's awesome!" and I said to her "you know what, you're right, cause my friend has said to me before that I definitely don't look like what I'm going through."

And I just wanna thank God that my cousin made me see things that way cause y'all already know that Lil red devil over my shoulder was getting ready to make me entertain the thought of "what if this," "what if that," and I can't, and I won't allow it, cause I'm **HEALED**!

And also, thanks to you, Mrs. Kathy, for reminding me as well that "**I AM COVERED**." I'll continue speaking that over my body each and every day.

Friends, there's power in "Spoken Words" Believe it!

FRIDAY, OCTOBER 27
Chemo Cocktail #7

Please uplift me in prayer as I prepare to receive another dose of this "pink" cocktail. Every treatment is a step closer to the finish line, but I also dread every treatment.

Especially that AC, Lord! Thank God it's over cause there was one day, I swear, as I sat in that recliner, I literally felt the poison going into my body. My nurse said it was my mind playing tricks on me. But no, that feeling was real.

So real that I couldn't help but cry that even Ashley consoled me by saying, "You've been doing so good; nothings gonna happen to you!"

And while they do prescribe anxiety pills, I haven't taken one till this day. I would much rather cry knowing that God's got me no matter what.

Thank you for praying for me, warriors, cause, at times, even Wonder Woman can't handle it all.

Love y'all.

FRIDAY, OCTOBER 27

Taxol 10/27

Taxol #3 is over and done with! Praise God, it was a success, although I was knocked out once that Benadryl kicked in.

Boi! My nurse was laughing, and the patients were like, "What did you give her??!?!?" Lol.

My favorite massage therapist Jill came to tell me she was leaving, and I was knocking down stuff tryna hug her. I'ma miss her so much. Eventually, one of us would say goodbye, but I didn't expect her to say it first. But I wish her luck cause she was a doll.

Today I also saw the nurse practitioner, and she said once again, as I already knew that the tumor is gone! And that there is no need to do scans right now because it's evidence that the chemo is working. But I'll definitely have them done later once treatment is over. The goal, of course, is to be cured, and as far as she's concerned, I am! It's funny how I could understand that much in between me passing out on her. Lol.

Overall, today was a great day; this morning, a gentleman saw Uta and me take pictures, and he said to us, "Can I take a picture of you two together?" And although he didn't press the right button and nothing came out, what he said to me made my day. He said, "I'm glad to see someone still making light of the situation because my mom is in denial and having a rough time," so I "preached" to him a little bit (according to Uta, lol). And I hope I was able to share an encouraging word.

God is good, Warriors! Even in the midst of our storms, He's still good.

Love always, Lina

SATURDAY, OCTOBER 28
Be Positive!

thetruthaboutCancer.com/gift-diagnosed-with-Cancer/

MONDAY, OCTOBER 30
Gifted Imagez

Today I was blessed to shoot with **Gifted Imagez**. Not only did they take some great shots, but the owner, Kevin, encouraged me to push my breast cancer shirts a step further.

It's amazing how some people can help you think above and beyond your vision.

Cause tonight, I'm definitely starting an Instagram page to promote my campaign and launch my book release.

Oh yes! This book is happening.

MONDAY, OCTOBER 30
Do You Trust Me?

This morning while thinking of a conversation I had yesterday with Kevin, I felt the Lord asking me, "Do You Trust Me?"

And one would surely think, "Well...duh, absolutely!" but why is it that sometimes we can trust God completely with one area of our life and be hesitant with the next??

Hello! Am I speaking to somebody today?

From the beginning of this storm, starting with the genetics test... I prayed and prayed, and the Lord gave me exactly what I wanted.

With the chemo, I remember Dr. K looking into my eyes, knowing I was in fear after she said, "there's a 2% chance of Leukemia and a 5% chance of having Heart complications" and after knowing the possibilities, I said, "Lord I trust you!"

Going back to the day I had my biopsy, I knew Dr. P already knew what it was, but still, I said, "Lord, I trust you!"

From the beginning, people have said all sorts of things about chemo, but still, I said, "Lord, I trust you!"

I could go on and on about this season and how I've had to trust God with the unknown. And after all these answered prayers, I still hesitate with other areas.

Now isn't that crazy!?!?

But this is true not only for myself but for many of us...

Many of us today are struggling with fully releasing some areas of our lives unto God; many of us will say, "Lord, I trust you," but still grab on tight to a particular situation. But God is saying, "Stop struggling, my dear, and allow me to take control of every and any Situation!"

Friends, He's proven himself to be faithful to us daily. He's worked out situations that we've deemed impossible. He's opened up doors and favored us time after time, so surely we must be able to trust Him with whatever it is He's asking us to release unto Him. Am I right?

While it is true at times that trusting God with the unknown Isn't always easy, we've gotta learn to release it all unto Him.

After all, He's never failed us yet!

Now let us pray.

Prayer to Trust More In God

"If you're praying about it, God is working on it!"

XOXOXO

TUESDAY, OCTOBER 31

Ain't It Funny

Hey everyone, it's 1 am, and I just had to tell myself, "Evelina remember you're in remission, and you need to take your behind to bed!" Lol

Man, this Taxol has been nothing compared to the A/C; however, my body was aching yesterday, but that's because I took Emil to the mall, and he gave me a workout. Lol, but other than that, I'm feeling myself. Like I've said before, I truly forget at times that I even have Cancer.

Like just a few minutes ago, I was changing my clothes, and as I was taking off my sweater, I thought to myself, "Man, I really don't wanna mess my hair up." **SMH**... crazy how quickly I forgot I was even wearing a wig! Then I was like, "What is around my neck?!?"... Duh! It was my glasses that fell off as I lifted my sweater. I forgot about them cause I never really wore my glasses till I started this journey, and now I'd much rather wear them because the contacts bother my eyes—the total opposite.

But yeah, just that quickly, I forgot all about you, Mr. Cancer. That means you're definitely not winning this battle! And you have no control over my life!

Well, tonight, I've titled this blog "Ain't it Funny" cause my Instagram is up and running. Yeah!

And I just have to smile because I had no plans to share my journey online. And even now, I still wanna keep a private profile. If y'all recall, when I broke the news to y'all, I said, "I am not sharing this with the world...cause everybody doesn't want your healing."

But the Lord is making me see that this journey is definitely not about me. And that this season right here had already been predetermined.

He already knew He was going to bump me into mylifeline.org; He already knew who my support team would be. He already knew that He was going to bring back my campaign, He already knew this would be my #1 seller! He already knew that photo shoot had a purpose. He already knew this was more than just a blog. He already knew there was no way that I was keeping this Glory to myself.

Man...look at God! His thoughts are definitely not our thoughts.

Amazing huh?

And as far as everyone not wanting my healing. I still feel the same way. But I believe if He's making this happen, then surely He's got me covered.

Love y'all.

FRIDAY, NOVEMBER 3

Loooord, please help me go to sleep. I've taken all ten of my premeds and I still can't shut my eyes. Or perhaps I don't want to, or maybe I just don't see the point in sleeping since it's already 7 am.

The Anxiety is real, my friends! Why am I always like this before treatment?!?! I don't know. But I still haven't taken any pills for it, and thank God my heart palpitations have stopped. During the A\C, I could feel my heart beating strongly every now and then at night. But praise God, it's over, and I'm not claiming anything over my body.

But guess what y'all?!! Yesterday was a productive day for me... which is why I'm surprised my behind is not yawning. What the heck! Where's that sleepy sand dust when you need it?!? Lol

OMG, now it's already almost 8 am. Honestly, there's really no point in sleeping now. I might as well get in the shower and get myself together cause they're just gonna drug me up anyway once I get there. Then I'll get all the sleep I need in that comfy recliner.

Love Y'all xoxo

FRIDAY, NOVEMBER 3
By The Way

In case I forgot, did I mention that at a recent event called The Pink Perseverance, Spirit of Hope Dinner/ Dance the guest speaker was not only amazed to know that I'm going through chemo, but she gave me a tight hug. Then she said something to the effect of, "Keep fighting. I can tell that you're a very strong woman!"

Her words of encouragement really touched my heart and it's amazing how others can see your inner strength.

> "Strong women don't play victim, don't make themselves look pitiful and don't point fingers. They stand and they deal."
> — Mandy Hale

SATURDAY, NOVEMBER 4
Taxol Day 4

Hey, y'all, chemo #4 was good yesterday. Although I was knocked out before she even administered it. Lol, and when I woke up, everyone in my room was gone! I was like, daaang,

I must've been sleeping hard as heck. I didn't hear a thing; I just remembered her tapping me to scan my bracelet, being that I was too out of it to verbally confirm my name and birthday. After that, I don't remember a thing!

Then I came home and slept the afternoon away. I woke up around 1 or 2 am to make some tortillas and played around on my new **IG** page. (I'm loving it) and chatted with my cousin Ricardo.

BTW did I tell y'all that my sister has dedicated herself to taking off every Friday to be by my side. Man, I'm telling you all these special gestures are all attributing to my healing… God has truly blessed me with a strong support system.

Again thank you all for your continued prayers. God is a healer!!! And I'm smiling today because He's been so so good to me.

Happy Saturday, love always and forever, Lina - Muah!

MONDAY, NOVEMBER 6
Effective!

Hi friends! Overall it's been a good week for me. Monday, I was in bed pretty much all day resting due to some minor aches here and there. Then on top of that, I found out we lost a family friend, so I've just been in "reflection mode," thinking of aaalllll the good times we shared together.

Maria... that was her name, an old neighbor of ours who was always at my mother's side, especially during my accident. Man, she was such a beautiful person. And, as a matter of fact, come to think of it, she was one of the very first people to point out that I was gifted in writing.

So I just wanna say thank you, Maria, for being an angel on earth and may God continue to comfort your family in this season.

Well, today's blog is titled "Effective," and believe it or not, I've had this one in draft mode for about four/five days now... back and forth Crazy, right?!? Lol.

But anyways, here we go.

While chatting with my godmother the other night regarding her testimony, I was immediately inspired to let y'all know that your testimony will always be "effective."

(This is gonna be a long one, so brace yourself, friends...)

Do you know that God has a way of using each and every one of us differently?!? He can take ten to fifteen people, put them through the very same thing, and still end up with ten to fifteen different "effective" testimonies. So don't you ever discredit your testimony, no matter how great or small. Because in some shape, form, or another, God is going to use you!

Let me highlight...

At the beginning of this diagnosis, I was introduced to an older woman at the church. She'd had a mastectomy. And at that time, the doctors believed that perhaps I'd be facing the same thing... But let me tell you how God used this sister ... she said, "I'm going to pray for you! You're gonna have a different testimony cause you're too young to have them cutting up on you like that. Therefore, I'm going to pray for you!" Now, look at me! Can't nobody tell me prayer doesn't change things. Not only did God use her to be an intercessor for me, but He also used her to elevate my faith.

And let me tell you, I oooh so needed it. Let us say..."effective!"

I learned from another survivor on her deathbed that "God is my ultimate Healer." I'm pretty sure you're thinking, "Well duhhh, Evelina, that's a no-brainer," but when you're facing Cancer, chemo, potential lymph node involvement, years of concern, brain scans, body scans, bone scans..ugh! You've got this mindset that I'm afraid to even write out. But I just thank God for using that sweet little grandma to remind me that God was my healer. And it was then that I began truly believing that I was walking confidently in my healing... say it with me, "effective!"

And from the third one, who had a 9 cm lump in her throat, God used her to tell me, "Get rid of every negative person and anything in your life that's causing you stress, Right now!" And that's exactly what I did; I began to encircle myself with people I knew would encourage, inspire, trust

God and know without a shadow of a doubt that I was going to make it. And what's the first thing my oncologist said after confirming my shrinkage?? "Your **IMMUNE SYSTEM** reacted to your **POSITIVE** attitude.

Now, scream it out loud!! "EEeeeeeffectiiiiive!!!!!"

Have a Blessed One.

Love Lina.

FRIDAY, NOVEMBER 10
Half Wayyyy !!

Hiii, everyone. Thank you so much for your continued prayers. Yaaay, I'm halfway there. Dec 29th is my last day for chemo.

Praise God. Please pray that all my scans come out clear. My oncologist said I may need radiation depending on if three lymph nodes come out positive. She has to double-check her records. But if the tumor was over 5 cm, that's another reason to do it since I'm keeping my breast. It's all cool, though; if needed, she thinks it'll only be five weeks. The most important thing to me right now is for my scans to come out all clear in Jesus's name. And for there to be no evidence of Cancer.

PRAISE REPORT

For every symptom Dr. K asked me if I had today, I answered **NO** too. She was surprised at swelling, heartburn, neuropathy, and some others, even my fingernail beds. She said some people's nail beds turn completely black, whereas mine, only the thumbs, were affected a lil.*Praise dance*

I'm sooo happy!! Lord, you are my everything!! I must be a cat with nine lives cause you always save me. And I can't thank you enough.

Love you all. And have a wonderful weekend. <3

P.S. my mom crocheted this beautiful rose for me. Xoxo

SUNDAY, NOVEMBER 12
God Held Me Together

Song of Inspiration:
"God Held Me Together" by Zacardi Cortez

Who else, Lord? Who else? For it's you and **ONLY YOU** who covers me and holds me together.

Be Encouraged.

MONDAY, NOVEMBER 13
Rewind

It took me a while to make the connection, but now I remember why I love this shot so much...

So let's rewind back to July. There I was, a nervous wreck for the first time, with my dad sitting in the Riverside Cancer Center waiting room. Shaking, waiting for my name to be called for genetic testing... A test that would lead the direction of my treatment. A test that would affect not only me but my family if Positive. Oh Lord, it was a struggle keeping it together at that time.

Suddenly, I got up, found the nearest restroom, locked the door, got myself together, then looked in the mirror and declared, "I'm **HEALED**, and I made it!"

And tonight, I say...thank you, Jesus! For giving me the strength to face this diagnosis, thank you, Jesus, for giving me the strength to smile. Thank you, Father, for giving me the strength to inspire. Thank you, Father, for giving me the strength to share this journey, and thank you, Father, for continuously healing my body... I trust your prophecy every day. I'm **HEALED**, and I made it!

#encourageyourself

WEDNESDAY, NOVEMBER 15
Oli

Nov 5th marked fifteen years since my aunt passed away from Breast Cancer.

She was so much like a second mother to me that some days I just secretly prepared myself for someone to tell me, "Oli was really your mother." I love my mother, and my mother loves me unconditionally, but so did my aunt Olivia. In fact, because of my aunt's friendship with my mother in grade school, my mother became friends with my dad's family. Yep, they go wayyyy back.

I'm just so thankful she cared for me when I needed someone to comfort me. My parents' divorce wasn't easy on me, so she stepped in and raised me for a few years without help from anyone.

Lol, I was just sitting here thinking about how much she loved church. I used to be so happy when my dad would come to visit me cause I would convince him to keep me home. My uncle would then say, "you betta let her go cause, you know, when you leave, she is going to church!" Lol Mann, my aunt would go to church morning, noon and night! Lmbo, I promise you, one day we went to like four different churches in a day! Lol.

And I laugh about that now, but I'm grateful for the values she instilled in me during those years. If it wasn't for her planting that seed, my relationship with Christ wouldn't be as deeply rooted as it is today. And even though I've changed churches, I can genuinely say the Church of Christ taught me to love my Bible.

Lol, wow! I also remember she was the queen of free clothes giveaways before I even could understand it myself. Lol, oooh, I wish she was still here to go to all the ones I hit up monthly. It's funny one day; out of the blue, I was like, maaan, where did I pick this up from?? My dad fusses bout these things, and my mom loves it because I do... then I was like, duh! Oli !! **BTW**, Don't sleep on it y'all! Cause some people give away some niiiice things, I mean some really nice things for **FREE.**

But yes, on top of aaalll that, her kindness, her smile, her strictness, her dreams! (get that from her too)... I'll always think about the first time I was left home alone with her after her surgery. It just seemed as though God set it up that way cause He knew I was scared, and many years later, I'd be part of a community that no woman ever wants to become a part of.

If I remember correctly, she asked me to sit next to her on the floor as she showed me her chest. And she explained what happened and how she had to wear a prosthetic in a special bra. **SMH** lol I remember once Bonita telling her, "ma! Fix your tittie," lol cause I think she came out with it all lopsided; she ain't care; it was funny to her. That's one thing I'll never forget, that she still kept her Joy despite her situation. And just like me at times, it never stopped her from living. So thank you so much, Tia, for being my role model.

All in all, there's sooo, so much I can say about you, Oli. Including how much your beautiful voice amazes me to this day. You taught me to love God even before I knew Him. You were so proud of all my accomplishments, and I remember even scribbling a drawing in church one day and how much that alone amazed you. "Look, look, look, Charles!" Lol (as she elbowed my uncle)

Thank you so much for loving me, and thank you so much for allowing God to use you to raise me. Thank you so much that even the song at your **FUNERAL** speaks to me today in the midst of my struggle. As Mrs. Dorothy, your best friend said, you knew the battle wasn't yours, and I'm learning it now.

Thank you, Tia! Thank you!!

Missing you, Evelina Xoxox

Song Inspiration: "The Battle Is the Lord's" by Varn Michael Mckay

THURSDAY, NOVEMBER 16

The Effects

Hi everyone. Thank you for your continued prayers. Sorry I haven't been writing like I normally do. On top of LinaImaging, I've been a Lil down some days. Taxol, I think tryna creep on me. So tomorrow Ima definitely let them know I've been experiencing some symptoms. So they can adjust the dosage.

Achy bones, poor circulation, shakiness, I've just been a Lil drained. But it just dawned on me, "duh!! Evelina, you had Lupron in addition to the Taxol." Right!! Cause chemo #1 made me feel the same way. But we'll see; Ima still report it, just in case.

Other than that, I'm ready for tomorrow. I took my 10 pm pills, packed my bags, and am looking forward to another one down. Ooooh, **BTW**, did I tell y'all my nurse said I was wild??!? Lol, but in a good way, of course. :) I guess because I'm always smiling, taking pictures, and walking around. But

I mean, I just refuse to let this get me down. Even today, I had to control my thoughts because my breasts feel funny and my chest a lil achy. And my mind just went straight to, "Ima ask them what is the stage, what if this, what if that...is that why she touches me on my other breast??" Just a bunch of things, and I had to tell myself, "Evelina, I'm pretty sure she would be really on top of you." Then I started thinking, "Is that why she always has this look that worries me when we talk about the scans???... y'all keep me in prayer cause I do my best to trust God and keep it together, but some days I do think about the results of all my testings. I said I wanna wait till it's all over, but I'm thinking bout asking her some questions on my next appointment. So please pray for me.

Well, it's 11:30 am, and tonight I can't hang :) I'm just so drained, and my hand is a Lil shaky.

But please know that I love you all and your support encourages me every day.

#HEALED!

THURSDAY, NOVEMBER 16

Yes!

Jesus turned, and seeing her said, "Take heart, daughter; your faith has made you well."

MATTHEW 9:22

FRIDAY, NOVEMBER 17
LIFE

Thank you for your prayers, everyone, praise God my numbers were good, and I received my treatment today.

Well, overall, it was a good day. This morning, I learned so much about life within those four hours at the center.

First, one of the patients came in for treatment even though her husband of 53 years died this morning. It was so sad; ontop of hearing how as a mother she choose for her son not to sit by her side but rather to remain outside. Oh, the heart of a loving mother. I'm telling yall, it was truly a sight, how she STILL came in to "fight."

My God!

Lastly, I also met a man with a history of heart complications; toe amputations and now, battling Cancer. Whew! he was sooo motivational, and with every word he spoke I just had to take notes.

He said:

"Your expectancy can be no greater than your attempt."

"You have to feed yourself!"

"I'm so grateful I'm full!"

And another thing he encouraged me on was when I was telling him how at one point, I asked God not to turn up the fire like Job because I've been through so much in my life. Cause I didn't think I could handle it, he said to me. "Don't bargain with God, don't be afraid for Him to use you. Let Him turn it up! It's part of your testimony." He was so funny and encouraging. I love the people I meet at treatment.

God is sooo good, my friends; despite our setbacks and heartbreaks, we must know He's working behind the scenes for our good.

Love you all xoxoxo

MONDAY, NOVEMBER 20
Happy or Sad

Hi everyone, I promised myself I'd write whether good or bad, happy or sad.

As usual, I managed to do some work today, but it wasn't long till I was aching. Today the aches are a Lil more intense. I've noticed even my appetite has gone down. I ate some boiled eggs and a Lil ziti, but I didn't even touch the soup I made. It concerns me because I wanna maintain my appetite, but I just don't feel like eating like I did at the beginning of chemo. (Pray for me.)

Besides my appetite, like I said, my legs ache. My mom massaged me, but I was still a lil weak when I stood. And at times, my arms and chest area ache too.

But the good news is... I'm only just a few more weeks till the finish line. Praise God for my pain tolerance and strength to endure this test.

Thank you all, Lina.

TUESDAY, NOVEMBER 21
A Rundown

Hi everyone.

How are you? Today was a great day for me. I actually did some work, went to the eye doctor, and hosted my family prayer call...all in a good mood with no aches and pains. Yeah!!

AND HOW WAS YOUR EYE APPOINTMENT?

Wonderful! Praise God she said there's no evidence of the ulcer and that the discomfort I'm experiencing is from the chemo...six more rounds and I'll be back to contacts!!! I really miss them, although, at times, I feel cute in my Coach lenses (lol, the only name-brand accessory I own) lol.

Reeeewiiiiind

Last weekend - I was blessed to attend the Women of Change Ministry play at Shiloh Baptist. My mom was one of the actresses, and she did an excellent job as Mary, the mother of Jesus. I also would like to thank Min. Perry and Sis. V for inviting me. I really had a wonderful time, and two of the sisters in the play gave me roses as a symbol of support in my fight. "Thank you, Father, cause you just keep surrounding me with all kinds of loving people in this battle."

Also, that afternoon, I visited my pastor/ coach. Please uplift Pastor George and his family in prayer that his heart may strengthen itself again. He's such a remarkable leader, and I've grown to love him like a father. If y'all only knew how grateful I am that God used him over the years to pick me up at a time when I was in deep depression. **SMH**. But God!

All in all, it was a wonderful day, and guess who God even used to encourage me this morning?? Navient! Can you believe that.??? Lol.

The bill collector was able to bring my loan current, minister to me, and on top of that, she closed out the conversation by saying, "And remember where your strength comes from!"

POWERFUL! Just powerful.

Love y'all, Lina.

THURSDAY, NOVEMBER 23

Thank You!

On this Thanksgiving Day, I am grateful to each of you for taking the time to follow my journey. Your support means the world to me.

I am strong in this season not only because of God but because of the people He's placed in my life to uplift me and to remind me of His goodness.

May His love continuously surround you.

Love, Lina. Xoxoxo

FRIDAY, NOVEMBER 24

In Advance

Yesterday I said, "Man, I wish we got a break from treatment like the workers who get a break!"

And, of course, without even thinking, I forgot that I need to be careful with my words because almost 90% of the time, when I speak, things come true (yeah, man, the power of the tongue).

It's crazy that I would even say that, let alone that I said it on Thanksgiving!! What the heck was I thinking??? (Someone, please throw one of Emil's plush balls at me, 'cause ya girl is tripping! Like seriously - she's out of this world tripping!)

That's why tonight my consciousness is bothering me... she's saying, "Evelina, don't say that! Cause being able to be treated is a blessing... you don't know how many people want to be in your spot! You don't know the number of people heart-broken with low #'s! you need to count your blessings, my dear! And even if you said it because you're tired, being sarcastic, or because you want your life back... whatever the reason, you've gotta watch what you speak... because the words you spoke yesterday can very well come true! So honey, don't you **EVA** repeat it!"

Mannn...that inner voice, I tell ya, lol sometimes she be getting on me!

But she's right, though, "we" cause it's not only myself who's guilty of it. We need to watch what we speak! And speak life over every and any situation of our lives. When in fire, speak life! When things aren't going our way, speak life! When things are going good, continue speaking life! C'mon now! I'm not only talking to myself here. I've got a life just like you outside of this Cancer into which I need to speak life. Friends, I'm with you too! We've gotta learn to always **SPEAK LIIIIFE!**

(Now, I don't know about you, but if I was wise enough to listen to that inner voice all the time, life would be sooo much better for me by now. But we live, and we learn. And It's all part of our grand testimony.)

So with that being said, I just wanna say thank you, Father, for my treatment today on Nov 24! And thank you in advance for the treatment of so many others as well. I know that you don't have to do it, but you do it because you love me, and as one sister said, you do it because you see "ministry" within me. Thank you! In your son's precious and holy name. Lina

#numbersarehigh! #readyfortreatment! #healed!

"The tongue has the power of life and death..."
Proverbs 18:21 NIV

FRIDAY, NOVEMBER 24
The Decision

As you all know, one of the biggest decisions I've had to make this season was a mastectomy or lumpectomy.

Yeah, to some, it's a no-brainer, but it was somewhat of a big deal for me. And not because I'm attached to my boobs or anything, but because having a mastectomy to me personally was a major **DECISION** that I simply did not want to make.

But praise God for answering my prayers, and thanks to my oncologist for confirming that reconstruction wasn't necessary. And that, for me, removing them wouldn't lower my chances of recurrence. (If that was something I was concerned about.)

Let me tell y'all, I'm so glad she confirmed that cause although I had made my decision, some people would still try to persuade me into a mastectomy.

But honestly, there are some decisions you just simply gotta make alone. Especially, **ESPECIALLY** when it comes to your body.

I mean, let's be real, who has to live with the consequences? Who has to endure the surgery? Who has to heal? Me!?! Seriously, at the end of the day, I have to look at myself in the mirror every day and say, "This scar is a reflection of **MY DECISION**!" Not a decision that anybody else made, but **MY DECISION,** cause if not, I may end up living with regret. (And who wants that?)

Even my mom said to me, "I simply can't comment on that one," when I asked her for her advice.

But anyhow, friends... to God be the glory cause I'm at peace. I trust my doctors, I trust this chemo, I trust that every living Cancer cell in my body has been destroyed, and I trust **MY GOD**!

The decision for my lumpectomy has been made, and I'm trusting God that I'm already **#HEALED**. In Jesus' name, **#AMEN**

> "You will know you made the right decision: you feel the stress leaving your body your mind. your life"
> — Brigitte Nicole

SATURDAY, NOVEMBER 25

Another one down! 11/24

Yaaaay!!!!! Another one down!!! I believe that leaves me with five more if I'm counting correctly... and I can't wait to bang that Gong. Hopefully, this time, I'm not drugged up like I was last time. Lol (thank goodness you all didn't see how long it took me to get myself together for that one take) smh

But yes, overall, yesterday was a blessed day despite the shift.

The **SHIFT**???

Yeah, due to the holiday, only 3 nurses were scheduled yesterday...So they had us all mixed up with different people... but that's okay cause God always knows exactly who to surround you with. And He placed me right among some beautiful people.

Patient #1 was diagnosed with Breast Cancer - beat that! Then ovarian - beat that! And now she just comes in for some preventative shots. She looks soooo beautiful, strong, and courageous. And she says she owes it to no one but God! Amen!

Patient #2 was paralyzed from the waist down, But God! She is **#Healed** and walking again!!! Now diagnosed with a rare form of blood Cancer. But before leaving, I said to her, "I'm claiming you are Cancer-free and already Healed!" And she said, "I receive it!" I love it; the same way these people inspire me with their strength and determination, I do my best to give back.

SUNDAY, NOVEMBER 26
Christmas Spirit

Hi everyone. Hope you had a wonderful Sunday. I didn't make it to church this morning, but yesterday I did fellowship with my church members decorating for Christmas.

I had a wonderful time, and the church looks so beautiful. Pastor Sophie has an eye for decorating, so the decors were unique.

But today, I've been lying in bed a lot. I've noticed that I'm usually tired the next day when I'm on my feet all day. Especially after treatment time... unusually, I also wake up with a nosebleed. I read online that Breast Cancer chemos can cause it, but my friend thinks perhaps my sinuses dried up, which caused it... but I've never bled that way before. But thank God we could control the bleeding after some pressure and a cold rag.

Now I'm preparing to soak in some Epsom Salt for these aches and pains... You would think lying in bed all this time would've relaxed me, but nooooo...

It's all good, though. I'm singing.

"I Smile" by Kirk Franklin / James Harris Iii / Terry Lewis / Fred Tackett

Love you all. And please pray for me. I have an oncologist appointment Tuesday at 10 am.

TUESDAY, NOVEMBER 28
The Stage

Heyyy Friends...

For the most part, my appointment went very well; other than that, my oncologist blurted out the stage.

Talking bout "I think you have stage..." **WTH**?!?!

Now my strength is a bit shaken and I'm doing my best to snap out of it. I specifically told her not to, but she talking 'bout she wanna be tough on me and that knowledge is power. Omg, I swear I could barely speak without my voice shaking after she did it. But she says that I've been doing so well with treatment that she believes my surgery will confirm it and that this stage means my treatment was delayed, but her aim is for a **CURE**.

Aaahhhh.

Friends, I really didn't wanna hear this; my plan was to make it all the way without knowing. I can say that I'm definitely not at death's door; otherwise, my treatment would've been a whole lot more aggressive. Praise God. But still!!!

My doctor is a trip, I tell ya! She asked me, "why wouldn't you wanna know about your body?" Giiirl cause it was my decision not to knooooow. Smh. **OMG**!!!

All I could say to myself was, "this ain't coming back, Evelina... this ain't coming back... no matter what the stage, this will never come back. In the name of Jesus."

Prayer Warriors uplift me in prayer; I need to guard my thoughts.

BTW, she plans to keep me on the Lupron for an additional five years, I'm guessing in addition to the ten-year pill, because studies have shown that women who do it this way at my age live longer.

Dr. K, Dr. K, I love you, but you don' messed me all up today.

"Sometimes you have to go through things and not around them"
The Fresh Quotes

WEDNESDAY, NOVEMBER 29
Thank you Sis. V!

What a beautiful song sent to me this morning by my sister in Christ, Sis. V.

An awesome reminder that "God Still Heals" by Kevon Carter

THURSDAY, NOVEMBER 30
Facing It!

It's 12:44 am, and I know I should be in bed, but some blogs I just gotta finish...

Well, friends, I'm over it and facing it today. In fact, I give her credit for holding it as long as she did for the four months she respected my wishes.

As I've said before, "it's amazing how others can see your inner strength" cause she already knew before I did that I could handle it. In fact, the staff themselves have been telling me how proud they are of how far I've come since day one.

You see, they knew that I would've fainted back in August (Seriously!). But what I didn't know is that this week I would be able to hear it, have my "Warrior Cry," and still be able to stand on "Solid Rock."

I guess it's because, after the emotional roller coaster, I had to stop and realize that regardless of the stage, I'm still **#HEALED**! Regardless of the stage, there's much to be thankful for!

> *"You gain strength, courage and confidence by every experience in which you really stop to look fear in the face."*
> — Eleanor Roosevelt

SUNDAY, DECEMBER 3
A Mess!

Hey fans

Wonder woman was a mess on Friday! They called the psychologist and the paramedics and strapped me up!

Not exactly, lol...but I was a mess! And for 1 bad day, they thought I was crazy. As if "I" wasn't allowed to have a meltdown?!?!? Geeeez.

Well, it all started like this:

As you all know Tuesday, I found out about the stage, and by Thursday, I was good... But then, The night before treatment, of all nights, when I had to take my pills at 10 PM and 4 AM, my cousin needed my counsel and the conversation convicted me, which in return escalated to me staying up till 6 AM. **SMH**.

Imagine... nooo sleep, steroids, menopause, emotions. Then the stage comes back to mind... **OMG**!!! Loord, help me!

But I just knew I had it under control, y'all; I just knew I did. But instead, I get to the center, and Ashley pumps more drugs in me and gives me the Benadryl... nooooo.

Then she tells me she called the counselor, and at first, I was cool with it but then eventually, all the drugs in me started making me ramble on and on... and The counselor looks at me like I'm crazy. Till I finally said, "I'ma write u a letter cause right now, I can't concentrate, and I'm making no sense." And of all the things she said that stuck out to me was "do u feel you've been faking your attitude?" Loord, why did she say that??? And I can't remember exactly how I answered her, but I know for sure I told her "no!"

Maannn emotions can mess you up! Never thought I'd crash this way. And I can't expect anyone to understand how that can happen to me, either.

But it's okay, they can say and look at me like I'm crazy, but I'm allowed a meltdown. I'm going through Cancer and a whole lot of things… I'm allowed a meltdown. And I don't feel sorry for it cause I'm human!

Heck, I have a lot on my plate…so one or two meltdowns out of the sixteen treatments is betta than most.

#incontrol #countdown #4more2go!

Goodnight.

WEDNESDAY, DECEMBER 6

Five Years

Buenas.

Thank you all for your prayers; I'm coming around.

Sunday, I was still a Lil jittery from treatment. I don't often feel this way, but my doctor said that some side effects can come from the recent Lupron. (But I'm sure my episode also contributed to my side effects.)

Anyhow. Five years!

Yep, I've titled this blog Five years cause that's how long I'll be menopausal. But why???? Well, because five years is the ideal time span, they want you Cancer-free, I believe. (Correct me if I'm wrong y'all?)

And usually, whenever I mention having to wait for my next baby, people always say, "just be happy with what you've got," or something to that effect...and I understand what they are saying cause my first reaction was, "Dang, five years! I'ma be 40!" Still, hey, we are going for the best preventative care right now. So who cares if I'll be 40?!?

Halle Berry did it! JLo did it! Mariah did it! "Yeah, but that's different. They can do that!" And?? I can do it too! :) My mama had me at 31 years. Then later, she had two more. And many other women have kids at a later age. So why should I let Cancer control my future? If she said five years. Then after five years, I'ma have lil "Lina."

On another note, wanna know what's funny? When I was younger, I always said, "I want a surrogate!" Had no idea where the $ was coming from, but I used to say that faithfully allll the time. Smh.

And this morning, I'm like, "wouldn't it be something if, in fact, my husband and I decide on going that route before the five years or after." Wouldn't it!!?! Especially because I spoke those words so much for no reason, and then to think about the manner in which it had to manifest would be mind-blowing.

So, friends, a lesson that can be taught here is to always, always, no matter what, be careful what you "speak." Cause sometimes we wonder, "man, why is this not happening for me?" or "Why is such and such happening this way?" & those are the times we have to sit back and reflect on our words... cause you never know, but perhaps you may have spoken some things in the past that you never truly hoped for.

#lessonlearned Love y'all.

THURSDAY, DECEMBER 7
From 0 to 100

I know it's 1 am. **Go to Bed, Lina!**

But I can't. I'm feeling some type of way...emotional, jittery, disoriented, I just can't think straight. And it has nothing to do with lack of sleep cause I've rested my mind pretty well this week.

But yeah, I just can't explain the feeling tonight. I've felt it before recently, but I can't describe it. All I know is that I told my mom, "I just wanna have a good treatment day," and

I promise y'all I will; Cause I want this over and done with.

And I know, I know, just the other day I said I'ma miss it. But tonight, I'm not feeling that way. Tonight I'm feeling like I want my hair to grow back, I want my job back, I want to move on with my life, I wanna make plans for next year, I wanna do what the heck I wanna do without treatment in the way, tonight I'm thinking… I just wanna live my **LIFE**.

I'm tired, y'all. Pray for me.

BTW the new medication I'm taking is Dexamethasone, and just like the Dr. said, mood swings are an actual side effect.

What a setup! Especially for a Libra.

FRIDAY, DECEMBER 8

James 1:12 CEV

My Morning Devo.

"God will bless you if you don't give up when your faith is being tested. He will reward you with a glorious life, just as He rewards everyone who loves Him."

How fitting.

Be Encouraged.

SATURDAY, DECEMBER 9

#4 Down!!!

#4 Down!! I had quite a few side effects to report, but today was a good day. No emotional breakdowns, except the usual rush in the morning. Lol, I swear I'm not a morning person. Then on top of that, I had to drop Emil off at daycare? But it's all good, I got there just in time, and the only thing I forgot to do was numb my port site. But after using an ice pack, I felt nothing at all. Ashley said it's because the port is above the muscle, and there's just a thin piece of skin above that area. Wow!

Moving on... Santa brought some gifts for the centeeeeeeeeer :)

I made a...

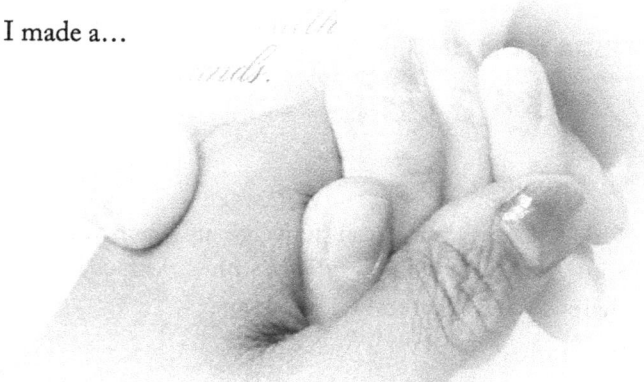

...Photo Frame for my Oncologist: Deut. 28:12 NIV (holding her hand).

4x6 Cards for the center that says "I Didn't Fight Alone" that the staff can sign and pass out to the chemo graduates, then color the ribbon according to the Cancer defeated.

And I also gave them wooden crafts that were given to me years ago. I had used some to make prayer boxes, and since the remaining were just sitting there, I wanted to donate them to a good cause. They loved it! Even the patients were asking what was in the box. Lol

My next task is to create a gift for the staff utilizing Emil's old milk cans that I saved :)). I love arts and crafts!

It would be a dream come true to do this all day and organize events for the center. So HR, if you're reading, I'm job hunting, lol.

Love y'all, and thank you so much for reading and your prayers.

#Keepingmyheaduphigh

MONDAY, DECEMBER 11
The Pill

Yaaaaayyy! Another year at the Newport News City Light Show!! And this time, Emil had a lil clue what was going on. Thank You, Healthy Families and Heike, for driving.

Well, friends, can y'all believe that last night was the first I ever took these anxiety pills. I swore I'd never take 'em, but I sometimes feel a lil jittery from treatment, and I don't like the feeling. Besides, from my understanding, all I'ma do is sleep all day with them, and that's not exactly the solution I'm looking for. So if I take 'em again, I'ma only do it at bedtime.

Then, this morning I did some work and took a midday nap. I wanted to do a lil more work, but my body was aching, so I took a nap. In fact, maybe that's what I need to do more of, "nap" to give my body all the rest it needs to recharge each day. Thank you all for your prayers and please remember to uplift me in prayer for this surgery. God's a Healer! I trust every single cell has been wiped away in the name of Jesus. We praise Him in advance!!!

Happy Holidays, Warriors.

Love y'all, and remember it's a blessing to be among the living. Xoxoxo

MONDAY, DECEMBER 11

As anxious as I am for this chapter to end, I pray that I never forget it and always share it.

#myjourney #hisgrace #blessed #mystory #testimony #healed

"You don't have to look like what you're going through!"

WEDNESDAY, DECEMBER 13
The Taxol Effect

"During treatment for Breast Cancer, you may notice some changes in the color or thickness of your fingernails or toenails or changes around the nail bed. Your nails may look bruised -- turning black, brown, blue, or green. These spots are not permanent and will grow out with the nails."

breastCancer.org/treatment/side_effects

Yep yep. My thumbs have bruised, and the edges of the other nails have done so too. One nail did lift and break in the middle, but my prenatals are helping with the growth, and the rest appear intact.

Recommendation: Paint them clear, no color, and nooo outside manicures. Oh yeah! No nail-biting as well. #sideeffects

FRIDAY, DECEMBER 15
Dying Empty

Hey, y'all!!

Don't get scared of the title! I promise I don't have bad news; seriously, it's some good stuff. Lol. Sooo...

Last Sunday in church, my Pastor spoke about how God will use different gifts within you in different seasons. And when she said that, I thought about how I've been writing soo much ever since Cancer came into my life. I mean, it's just been so therapeutic for me. And even in the past, whenever I went through rough seasons, I always wrote so many letters to God. (Pastor George can testify to that, lol.) So honestly, not only do I have two books within me, but I actually have three books cause the third one is already written and waiting for me to finish.

I have:

    Healed: My Journey From Cancer to Survivor
    A Better Woman: 35 Ways to Loving Him Right
    Dear God: The Diary of A Baaad Girl

Omg, I looove writing! And just a few weeks ago, I was even given the opportunity to write a company bio for a client. I was sooo nervous! Believe it or not, I've never written for that audience before, but when Catina took a look at it for me and said, *"You did great!"* I knew then I had the seal of approval. (She's an amazing editor) and then my client said, *"Evelina, that's awesome!"* And I'm like, Catina's right! Doors are opening in areas I never dreamed of.

And honestly, it's not even about the money y'all!!! (Although being on Oprah and Lifetime would be nice, lol.) It's about inspiring someone. It's about changing lives, and most importantly, it's about dying empty with allll my dreams completed.

TTYL Pray For Me xoxo. #treatmentday

> "Don't go to your grave with your best work inside of you. Choose to die empty."
>
> TODD HENRY

FRIDAY, DECEMBER 15
Transparent

Since I'm keeping a record of everything, I just wanted to share the letter I wrote to the center after my "meltdown."

Dec 5th

Good morning J!

Sorry, I meant to write to you yesterday, but I was still a Lil jittery from treatment.

First of all, I just wanna say that I absolutely love the center. I knew nothing about Cancer Care before being diagnosed, but Riverside promised that they would walk with me every step of the way, and they've done just that, Hands Down!

Where do I begin....:)

At 35, I've been through several health issues than the average. In my senior year of High School, I was hit by a car; in fact, I was literally one bone away from ever being able to walk again. But praise God, cause from crawling, wheelchair, walker, and cane, He beat the statistics and today I'm a walking miracle!

Then in my 20's, I contracted H Pylori and needed a blood transfusion...Till this day, I remember my doctor shaking his head in disbelief at all the backed-up blood within me... unexplainable...how is she even still alive? But I knew it was nothing but the grace of God.

Now 34, diagnosed with Breast Cancer. "J", it wasn't easy hearing the diagnosis; in fact, I asked my parents, "why is it always me??" But eventually, I got myself together and started seeing the blessing in the midst of my storm.

And from day 1, I told myself, "regardless of the Stage, I will be **HEALED***." And yes, it may sound silly not knowing to some people, but that's the way I wanted to carry out "***MY HEALING*** *process."*

Cause I knew I'd be worried bout statistics instead of focusing on being cured. I just wanted to be happy, to inspire, to be positive, to be inspired, and to focus on the man above who can do all things. So imagine the thoughts running through my head when it was revealed!?!

Then by Thursday morning, I thought I was okay...I had realized she didn't do it out of disrespect but more so to strengthen me.... she's seen how far I've come since day one, so she did what she thought was best, in her opinion, to help my curiosity.

But even with that determination, I guess in the back of my mind, I was still thinking, "oh Lord, I have stage such and such," "oh Lord, this increases my chances for this "... I hope I'm making sense today, cause I'm not a crazy person and I've **NEVER** *faked my attitude with y'all. (Cause when you asked me if I've been faking, that really made me feel some type of way)*

[I'm not mad at all with Dr. K. She's an awesome person whom I believe saw my inner strength. She believes in my healing regardless of the stage, and for that, I love her.]

Rewinding to Thursday's events...

Of all nights I had to take my pills...the Lord sent my godbrother for counsel. I was up till about 5 am listening to him, then up for the rest reflecting.

But that's another story cause I'd like to treat the center like a workplace. Meaning I leave all my troubles at the door and only focus on my healing. But insomnia, menopause, Dexo, Benadryl, and whatever other drugs y'all give me brought up a wave of emotions, especially after you changed the topic about the stage. It sent my emotions flying everywhere.

"J"... I don't wanna look like a maniac; I hate that feeling, especially in front of other people.

Next time, let's take it in a private room. Cause in this season, I'm dealing with so much, and if I just so happen to talk about other things for whatever reason, I don't wanna do it in the open...thank you.

Another reason I feel it should be done privately is because at the last minute, my dad had to bring me. We lost my oldest sister in '05, and now I'm sick, so you can imagine this is hard on my family...

That's why not knowing the stage was also something I wanted in order to help me stay emotionally stable. I didn't want my family to worry about me so much... and I know he was also eavesdropping Friday, but because I wasn't thinking straight, I failed to let y'all know I didn't want him near.

Aaahhh, I'll be sooo happy when this chapter is over. Sometimes dealing with so much and Cancer takes a toll on me. I'm human, "J"! Some days I'm going to crash, and Friday, for whatever reason I hate, was a bad day for me. I apologize, but then again, I don't, because I'm allowed to have days like these; I should know that I'm allowed to cry; I'm fighting for my life right now... and Cancer ain't the only problem that we as patients deal with from day to day.

So there you have it! The "wild child" :) had a breakdown Friday, but I guarantee you that she's had her "warrior cry" and is determined to pick her head back up again and finish strong. Four more treatments!!!

Love y'all. Xoxo, and thank you, Soo, much in advance for your understanding.

Evelina

FRIDAY, DECEMBER 15
The Baaad Girls

This season, God's asked me to "release" many things. Some for a moment and others for a lifetime.

And among my "moments" is "The Baaad Girls," an inspirational group I founded five years ago with my dear friends Jenn and Tynia.

THE BAAAD GIRLS, HUH?!? WELL, WHAT KIND OF GROUP IS THAT?!?

Lol, let me just say it's not the kind of "Baaad" you're probably thinking of. :)

On the flip side, our Baaad Girls are all single ladies with a heart's desire to be married. They know that God is able and faithful to make their dreams come true.

In their season of preparation, they learn to be patient, to **SHINE** (Matthew 5:16), and to trust in His perfect timing. They walk the walk of faith, trusting God all the way, and people look at them and say, "Mann, She's Baaad!"

Yes! I love my BGs xoxoxo. Not only are they an encouragement to me, but it's a blessing being able to remind them to believe in the Promises of the Lord versus the opinions of the world. (Luke 1:45) (Cause I tell ya, people can be so judgmental when it comes to relationships. And it's great to have a group that will not make fun of the vision God has placed within you.)

SO HOW DO Y'ALL ENCOURAGE?

Through Facebook Postings, Yearly Retreats, Bridal Shows Socials, Conferences and Testimonials.

Yess testimonials!!

Thank you, ladies, for carrying the torch for me in this season.

The Baaad Girls is such an amazing group and I thank God for birthing it in me.

FRIDAY, DECEMBER 15

Amen

"You are a fighter, a survivor, a woman of faith and strength. You are a tough opponent for any challenge. Even the big "C" is no match for you, because you belong to an even bigger "C"..."
Unknown

TUESDAY, DECEMBER 19

Taxol Week 10

Thank you all for your prayers. Taxol #10 was a success. Thank God they cut my steroids cause I felt much more relaxed on my way to treatment.

The only thing was that I misplaced my port's seal, so I had to improvise. (Ghetto!) Lol, so I cut a plastic bag and taped it on my chest. I told Ashley don't laugh at me! And she assured me I wasn't the first. Lol Hey! Whatever works. Huh :)

You guys, I'm getting close to the end!!! Two more, and I'm done. Now I need ideas for my last treatment, how should I celebrate??? Help!! I want something unique to do at the center. If you have any suggestions, please let me know.

O yeah! I also saw Dr. K on Friday, and thank goodness she didn't discuss my meltdown. That would've been awkward. But I know she was like, "get that crazy girl off them meds!!" Lol. And by the way, she loved my gift; it's already hanging in her office.

WHAT'S NEXT???

Well, she's done all she can for me regarding chemo. So now it's time to set up surgery for January (of course, I'll have to finish chemo first), But for surgery, I'll have the port removed, whatever lymph nodes gotta go, and the area that was affected gone bye-bye (I believe).

Then we'll take it from there for the next phase of treatment. (radiation)

Yes!! I'm almost to the finish line with chemo. Praise God! and Thank you all for walking with me every step of the way.

HOW YOU FEELING THIS TREATMENT??

So far, minimal side effects. I felt a lil disoriented and weak on Sunday as I was buckling Emil in his car seat. And then, that midnight, I had a nosebleed. It scared me! But God is still good, and He still sits on the throne.

I'm #Healed In the name of Jesus, I'm Healed! And knowing the stage is not affecting me anymore.

Love you all, and thank you for following my journey.

TUESDAY, DECEMBER 19
Transparent Part 2

In response to my email, the counselor said:

Good Afternoon!!

By the way, I have seen "crazy or a maniac," and you are far from either of those! Your attitude is inspiring and is exactly what helped you overcome all that you have.

I just registered for your blog, and when I get a min, I will definitely check it out.

Nothing but love, "J".

THURSDAY, DECEMBER 21
Within Me

"God is within her, she will not fall"
Psalm 46:5 NIV

FRIDAY, DECEMBER 22
Making It!

One of the things I'll never forget is the nurse at diagnostics telling me, "I can't tell you that it's gonna be easy, but what I can tell you is that you are gonna make it!"

Praise the Lord cause here I am, alive, breathing, full of life, smiling, I had my ups and downs at times, but she was right; I Made It!

Going through chemo wasn't as scary as I thought. The Riverside Cancer Center was a blessing. From diagnostics, my Navigator, my oncologist, my nurse Ashley, my 2nd nurse Amanda, my social worker, my vital nurses, my music guy :), my dietitian, admin, my masseuse, even down to all the roommates I've met. I was tremendously blessed along the way. And next week is going to be bittersweet.

Heavenly Father, thank you for holding my hand every step of the way. The smile and bravery I displayed were aaaaall you shining through me. And if it had not been for me knowing your healing power, I don't know how I would've made it. Just as the words in the song "Never Would Have Made It" by Marvin L Sapp says, *"I never (Never would have made it) No, I never (Never could have made it without You)."*

Lord, you get all the honor and glory this season. . I love you for holding my hand once again and bringing me through another challenge. I want more of you, Lord; I want to experience everything that you have for me. I love you, in your son's precious name. Amen.

P.S. Today, they had about three graduations!!

Cancer is not a death sentence y'all, many people make it...so tell someone you know battling tonight, "Keep the Faith!"

FRIDAY, DECEMBER 22
Taxol Week 11

Taxol Week 11 was very uplifting. The perfect day in prep for my celebration next Friday.

As you can see, I was in the holiday spirit. Santa's lil elf :)) bringing gifts, smiles, Snapchat and even my mom and my sister came to be with me. What a joyful occasion!

Ashley loved the gift mom made her, a yellow bonnet w/ matching shoes and a diaper cover. **OMG**, Kenna Brooke is gonna be the prettiest Lil baby in the world. Xoxox.

HOW WERE YOUR VITALS?!?

As usual, my vitals came out good; praise God, 100% oxygen! Yay baby! And Even though that scale ain't going down, my Navigator Elizabeth said I've lost weight and looking good...and you know what I told her. "As funny as this sounds *Cancer Brought Me Life!"

Seriously, it did! I mean, I used to wear makeup and stuff before at times. But after being diagnosed, I made it a point that I wasn't gon' look like what I was going through. And thanks to the American Cancer Society, I "looked good and felt better!"and had all the confidence I needed to know that no matter WHAT, I was gonna make it.

The support has been real y'all. Even the patients encouraged me through testimonies, encouragement, bravery, determination, and friendships.

As a matter of fact, a dear roommate graduated today, Mrs. Blanca. I still remember the first day I met her; she said, "How come you didn't lose your hair?" Lol. I was like, "this ain't my hair! This a wig!" Aww, Mrs. Blanca, she even gave my mom and I a bracelet from her country for good luck. Praise God for her recovery; she is so excited to be singing in her choir again, hallelujaaaaaaah!!! Singing a joyful noise unto the Lord!

This journey is surely bittersweet. I don't know what ima do with my Fridays, but I know I'm ready to move forward to the next phase.

Thank y'all for your prayers. One more y'all, yay!!!

FRIDAY, DECEMBER 22
Not My Strength

"Your strength in this season is remarkable."

That's what everyone seems to be telling me. And although I'm flattered, and it gives me great joy to hear; I just gotta say, "it is not my strength, but the strength of the Lord" hallelujaaaaaaah.

Friends, I've said it repeatedly; I honestly don't know how I would've made it without Him. How do people go through such a trying season without Him? How can He not be in the equation when you're going through a storm? How?!?

Lord, I'm so grateful for knowing you; I'm so grateful to be alive. I'm so grateful that I can say it shrunk!!!! I'm so grateful my last chemo is Friday. I'm so grateful for the love and support this season, and I'm so grateful that you love me and continue to use me for Your glory and your honor. Thank you, Father, thank you. One more down till surgery. May every Cancer cell be gone. May they see nothing and be amazed by your healing power. You can do it. I have no doubt that I am **HEALED**. I am **HEALED**. I've been **HEALED**! Thank you! Thank you. In your son's precious name, we thank you for the strength you've given me to uplift others, encourage and let them know that you are the mighty physician.

Thank you, for I know that your healing doesn't stop here; it continues covering me for the rest of my life. And it covers everyone who's reading this. In your son's precious name, we receive it. Amen.

> *"I Can Do All Things Through Christ Who Strengthens Me"*
> Philippians 4:13 NKJV

TUESDAY, DECEMBER 26

The "Gift"

This year I'm not only thankful for the gift of **LIFE** but for the gift of **WRITING**.

MyLifeLine has been such a tremendous blessing to me this season. Not only because it's therapeutic, but because it brought me **YOU**! (My Support System). Thank you.

Knowing that y'all actually take the time to read my writing is encouraging. Cause I never in a million years would've thought that my story would capture the hearts of so many Thank you!

I love writing, as you can see. My cousin tickles me; he said, "Oh man, if someone has to start from the beginning, they've gotta go wayyyy back cause you've written sooo much!" Lol. He said sometimes he may miss a few days and gotta catch up with the entries I've written. Lol.

OMG!! I love writing so much that I never even realized the countless journals I've gone through over the years. Even in church, I'm writing and posting sermon notes on Facebook. At work, I remember just pausing to write a revelation on any notepad I could find. Then the Lord must've said, "It's time! You need to start sharing your gift," cause about five years ago, after losing my job, I started writing "Letters of Encouragements" to my Baaad Girls.

And then, I started getting so many responses similar to Mrs. Kathy's below, stating how my writing was so encouraging. I even remember another friend asking me , "where do you get this stuff from?" Cause she's known me since '97 but never seen me write like this. Heck! I never knew that God was, in fact, using me with this gift till one day, I had finished reading something I had written, and I was like, "Wow! That's definitely not me! These words are not mine but yours, Lord."

And now look at Him! Exposing my gift in the form of a blog! A "Cancer" blog, at that. Wow! Just the thought of it makes me think about how amazing **HE** is. Because automatically hearing the word "Cancer" brings the word "depression" to my mind, so to be sharing my story with anyone else but **HIM** shocks me at times.

So that goes to show you, friends, this journey definitely ain't about Me! But it's about Him reminding us that He's the Healer! He's the way-maker! He's mightier than Cancer! He wants to fight all our battles.

So Lord, I just thank you this morning for the "Gift of writing" and for bringing MyLifeLine to me. They have been such a tremendous encouragement to my life, and I thank you, Mrs. Kathy, for your **TIME**! Dear Lord, what an honor to have her following my journey. What an honor to have You using me to encourage and draw souls unto you. What an Honor! They see now that you are indeed "**SUPERNATURAL**," and there's nothing impossible for you. I mean, **NOTHING**! So please, I ask that you continue to bless the work of MyLifeLine and all its efforts. For they are nothing but amazing people in your son's precious name Amen.

Yes, Mrs. Kathy, it's true...If you only knew how my eyes light up when I tell others about you. Your time means the world to me. I love you. **XOXO**.

Thank you.

Dear Evelina,

The week has finally arrived, your FINAL CHEMO TREATMENT this Friday! I have been so inspired by your strength, faith, and determination during this cancer journey. I know the journey does not end here, but it's a perfect time to pause & CELEBRATE all you've already been through! I will think of you & wear pink on Friday.

Hugs, Kathy at MyLifeLine

FRIDAY, DECEMBER 29

Merry Christmas

I'm so sorry. Amid the holiday hustle and bustle, plus the side effects, I forgot to say Happy Holidays to my faithful followers. I love you all for encouraging me and for giving me your time. Each and every one of you is a gift to my life. I love you.

SO WHAT YOU BEEN UP TO, LINA?!

Well, Sunday, I made it to church, praise God. And praise Him because our pastor, my life coach, who has also been sick, surprised us Sunday morning. The #HealingPower is real! He's getting stronger every day. I declare it. And His wife gave a beautiful testimony of how He's the perfect gift. It was sooo touching, the perfect example of how God wants us to praise our mates in public. And to acknowledge the gift that He's given us in the form of a soulmate. That's the kind of marriage that every Baaad Girl desires. As far as side effects later that day, I was drained. I think it's because, at times, my body gets a Lil tired from sitting down for long periods. But it's all good. I'm still alive!

Then Monday, Christmas Day, I was exhausted that morning again. The **TAXOL** must've been really hitting me. But I was straight once our gathering around 4pm started. My family had a great time together, and my lil sister cooked a wonderful dinner. She's all about family, unity, and getting down in the kitchen. So if you need a caterer, contact my lil sis! She makes these egg rolls that our mom Nita taught her to make as a kid that are the **BOMB**! I remember once they asked my niece, "where is your favorite place to eat?" and she said, "My mommy's house," and she's right cause whatever she wants, my sister can make it! Chinese Food – she can make it! Italian – she can make it! Anything these restaurants offer, she can make it! That's something she picked up honestly from both my parents... now me!

Yeeeaaah, that ain't my thing, I used to be into making casseroles, but I hate being in the kitchen. I tell anyone upfront, "that ain't my art!" I'm thankful I have my family to keep up with my diet restrictions this season. Cause my art is graphics and writing! Lol. Yes, Lord! So ask me about a flyer, then we can talk.

Yep, so after a great time Monday, at around 9 pm, the discomfort in my legs started again, and I called it a night. It's funny how good I've been handling the chemo that even my family sometimes forgets that I'm going through it. Cause I heard one of them ask, "what's wrong with her?" And my mom was like, "She gets like that sometimes from the meds," but just as I sometimes forget that I have Cancer, they do too. So that night, I believe I slept early after my mom rubbed my legs with Vicks.

Then Tuesday, we did a balloon release for my grandmother. She died the day after Christmas last year, and it was so beautiful.

But other than that, y'all, I've just been taking it easy since the last treatment. One of my Pink Sisters has encouraged me to rest because I sometimes share my symptoms with her. (BTW, did I tell y'all she's a nurse??) Cause sometimes I'm always on the go and so stuck on the computer that I never take the time to truly rest. So I've been resting to help with the fatigue, to help with the achiness and my nose bleeds, the menopause I must learn to get used to for the next couple of years, and to help with the circulation in my body.

A much-needed rest, away from everything, as I prepare to end chemo and go into the next phase, surgery. (To remove whatever lymph nodes, the port, and the affected area) keep me in prayer as I allow my body to rest so that these symptoms can quickly begin to leave my body, in Jesus's name.

One more treatment y'all!!!!! I don't hear ya?? I said one more treatment y'alllllll...lol. No more chemo in the name of Jesus. Yes!

FRIDAY, DECEMBER 29
The Day!

When I first got diagnosed, I remember my sister saying to me "we hope for the best, but prepare for the worst." And I said to her, "what worst?" Cause I ain't going nowhere.

And now that I think about it, I was actually prophesying over my **LIFE**! Saying, "Dear Lord if you can use anybody, use me! Use me, Lord. You know you can use me!"

Especially after the nurse at diagnostics said to me, "You are going to make it!"

Yes, chemo wasn't easy; I had my days, especially when I just knew I felt that A/C was going through my body. I know I wasn't going crazy; I actually felt I could feel something that didn't belong in me going down through every part of my body...But although I felt that way, I knew chemo was the choice I made to help me survive. So I managed to handle the season the best I could.

I came to treatment 90% of the time with a smile on my face, taking pictures, blogging, asking questions, making friends, and being inspired. I just loved it so much, and Ashley was my angel. I will never forget her patience with me; Kenna is Blessed to call her mommy.

I told Miss Kim that leaving y'all is bittersweet. "I feel so sad.

I really liked the center. The ambiance there is exactly the type I like working in, and I enjoy awareness. I'ma miss everyone. Hire me! I, too, wanna encourage even more patients and uplift their spirits with my gifts. My sister looked at me yesterday like I was crazy when I said, "I'm a miss Ashley and Amanda" She was like, "What the Heck! You betta be happy", and I am so happy to have come to the end of this phase but loved treatment days! Cause if y'all know me well, I'm not just sitting there quietly. I talk, talk, talk, that even once Greg said after I asked him for some headphones so that I could attempt to be "quiet" something like, "those headphones are no good if you keep talking," or something like that and he was right, not even that worked. Lol, he had both Ashley and I laughing. Then I was knocked out by that Benadryl! Man, that stuff was strong; it even made me miss my favorite roommate, Mrs. Blanca's graduation.

I truly Love the Riverside Cancer Center because they made a promise to me and fulfilled it! A promise to walk with me every step of the way...even on my bad days, even when I was a mess at treatment, they held my hand and helped me pick my head back up. Thank you, "J"!

Thank you for your hugs, Amanda. Thank y'all for the snacks and encouragement. Thank you, Mrs. Adele, for the extra flavor you bring to make this such a loving environment.

Thank You, Dr. K, for being my chemo momma and for your support and assurance. I still remember the day you drew out the chemo plan, and I looked at you, then you looked at me and said, "but that is not you! You are none of these things..." In other words, you were saying trust the process, and I just thank God for you cause with you, my life was in good hands. Even if you do wanna make me an "old woman" for the next five years. Lol, I trust you!

Man, I can't believe this day has finally arrived. It seemed like forever thinking about sixteen treatments. But with the Riverside staff, starting with Dr. N, who took action, as well as Dr. P, and Dr. C, who said to me, "Mrs. Johnson, I don't see no expiration date on you, and even if I did, only God knows." And my primary care doctor, who wanted to pray with me after my appointment, and the admin staff here for gifting me my "Super Cape!" which I wore proudly. My family for walking this journey with me, never leaving me alone, and for you, all my faithful followers on MyLifeLine who love and support me. All of you have been my cheerleaders along the way...oh, and how could I ever forget my pink sister Shawnna. I will never ever forget you calling me on your first day of chemo to encourage me. You have been my angel, and I repeat after you, "we got this girl!"

Thank you all. Now, let's do this!

FRIDAY, DECEMBER 29
Morning Message

"I refuse to look like what I'm going through!"

EVELINA

SATURDAY, DECEMBER 30
Hooray!

Last Day of Chemo!!!

SUNDAY, DECEMBER 31
Surprise!!!!

Sooo they got me y'all! My family don' managed to surprise me for the first time. Cause I definitely was not expecting a victory dinner.

In my mind, I was just thinking about this chemo being over and done, the 15th with Dr. K, the surgery, and possibly having a lil something, something to celebrate. But it never crossed my mind that my family would be planning anything for me.

Especially because I'm always coming up with ways to celebrate and decorate. Allowing them to even plan my baby shower was hard enough!

But today, I had no clue whatsoever what they had up their sleeves. And it was perfect! The decor, the planning, the intimate setting, the food! When I tell you they got me good, they got me real good. :) Lol.

And what's funny is that I **NEVER** really saw chemo too much as an act of bravery the way they did. I saw it as doing whatever I had to do to get better. Although I did feel some type of way when Dr. C said, "Would you at least hear what the chemo Doctor has to say?" Cause I was afraid, from everything, I'd ever heard about it. And all I wanted was for him to remove the mass and keep it moving... But nooo, things didn't pan out that way cause life ain't always easy. And the rest...well, God used me. But still, I never looked at it as an act of bravery. I just did my treatments with lil complaints.

Although there was this one time, while I was going through the motions with my hair loss, my dad told me, "Just stop complaining and do your treatments!" and I thought, "How insensitive of him!" But when I think back on it now, I remember the lyrics of the song "I Won't Complain" by Reverend Paul Jones

"I ask a question, Lord
Lord, why so much pain?
But He knows what's best for me...
So I'll just say thank you, Lord
I won't complain."

And He was right. Amid the side effects, I just had to keep thanking the Lord despite what I was going through. Cause many people wished they were in my shoes, despite how bad it may have seemed. Or some were scared to even give it a chance because of the side effects.

But my word of encouragement for those who are scared is to trust God. Hearing the word chemo scared the heck out of me. Many people told me all kinds of things. "Chemo not good for you," "you're gonna be frail," blah, blah blah...all sorts of opinions. But trust God if you're leaning towards it.

Losing my hair was probably the most emotional stage of the chemo treatment "I" received. The fatigue from the A/C drained me (I won't lie), but I pressed through, and the eye ulcer from the first treatment almost scared me. But just as soon as I changed my perspective and put in my mind that living in fear was not gonna be my story, my immune system responded to my attitude. And here I am today! Smiling and celebrating God's miracle with my family and you all.

Treatment doesn't end here. I still have surgery, five more years of Lupron, and ten years of a preventative pill. But today, my family celebrated my most significant achievement in this journey, and I thank them for never leaving my side.

Love Always, Evelina.

TUESDAY, JANUARY 2
The End.

Happy New Year!!!

Hope everyone had a blessed one. Wish I could say mine was great. But then again, despite whatever, I still have to say it was blessed cause I'm still here to tell it! Many people didn't even open their eyes this year and never had a chance to ring the bell, so it was still blessed.

SO HOW YOU FEELING LINA?!?

Well, I've been pretty much lounging allll day. I've had a nosebleed, bone ache, fatigue, the usual. (Although most of it I made it worse on myself by doing too much) But Tylenol has seemed to help, thank God. And Thank God for my sisters cause they helped me out with Emil.

As always, thank you all for your continued prayers. This year will be nothing like the year before. One successful surgery coming up!

WEDNESDAY, JANUARY 3
Farewell

Well, I can't explain how I felt on the last day. I wasn't in tears or maybe as happy as I should've been. Instead, I was thinking: finally, I'm closer to surgery and ready to see what my breast will look like. Lol.

I'm being real with y'all. What exactly does cosmetically pleasing look like? And how many lymph nodes are coming out??? Those thoughts were running through my mind, in addition to hearing them say, "Every Cancer cell is gone!"

That's all I can think about right now. And the fact that the journey at the bell still continues when others see it as the end.

But anyway, on my last day, I was greeted by glove balloons that said "High five," "Last day of chemo," and streamers. It was so sweet.

The only difference in my treatment that day was how I took my steroids. (Due to a fluid shortage in the country, many hospitals are administering medications orally or manually with a syringe.) Anything to cut back on fluids because some hospitals have had to turn away patients. So please pray that this problem will soon be resolved for those still in treatment.

Other than that, as usual, I was knocked out. Although I had tremendous family support that day. Everyone was taking turns visiting me in the room, and I wasn't honestly up for it, for all I wanted to do was sleep and ring that bell.

Cause I was aaaalllll drugged up! Lol.

Oh yeah! Due to the changes in treatment, it took a Lil longer to administer meds. :(For me, it was fine, but of alllll the days when I asked everyone to be there between 12:30-1pm. I don't think I rang the bell till about 2 something.

But in the end, they were all happy to see me give my speech and ring that bell seventeen times. Lol, One for the victory and sixteen bangs for sixteen treatments! And the clinic was so happy with my memory book gift. Next time, I'll have to take pictures of it to share it with y'all.

And the most touching part is that Shawnna came to see me. God Bless her; we've got this!

Aww, man, I'ma miss Fridays, but praise God, no more chemo!!! Yessss!!

THURSDAY, JANUARY 4
Neuropathy

Hi friends!

Praise God, it's Thursday, and my chemo days are over. Woohoo!

No more waking up at 4 am. I repeat, No More waking up at 4am. Yes!

Well, I've been doing okay so far, and each day gets better. The only thing I'm dealing with now is the neuropathy in my fingers and toes.

But I'm managing to catch up on some work and tomorrow I'll focus on a significant project. Doing my best to finish what I can before my surgery. Cause once I have it, I'll be in recovery.

Sure the sensation bothers me a little. But I'm sure within a few days, it'll go away, especially with chemo being over and increased rest as recommended.

Besides that, I'm feeling fine, and the 15th (oncologist visit) can't get here fast enough.

Thank you all for your continued prayers.

Oh, Looord, not another hot flash! Smh.

Goodnight, and I love y'all xoxo

SATURDAY, JANUARY 6
The Wig

Morning humor.

Woke up this morning and the first thing Emil does is throw a wig at me. (Dang!) Lol, #priceless.

WEDNESDAY, JANUARY 10
The Wait

Hi friends!

Soooorrrrry I haven't written in a while. Just been taking some time to myself to enjoy life without chemo! Amen.

On the 15th, as I said, I'll be seeing Dr. K, and my surgical consult has been pushed to the 23rd. Ugh! (I'm hoping that'll change to an earlier date).

But in this waiting period, I've been catching up on work, and I started my workout plan today.

Working out during chemo wasn't advised because I had to do my best to maintain a steady weight. (Cause chemo meds are made according to your weight)

Also, my hair is steadily growing, and my body is feeling back to normal. I'm so thankful for the energy God's given me to wake up every day and keep pushing forward.

I know I'm **HEALED** 100%. Just want this surgery to be over and confirm the miracle of God's healing power.

I love you all. Thank you so much for your support and encouragement.

TUESDAY, JANUARY 16
The 15th

Hi friends! Thank you all for your prayers yesterday. Overall it was a wonderful visit.

I was all over the place tryna say hi to everyone. :) lol (**OMG**, I love the center :))

Because my appointment was a bit behind, it all worked out in my favor, and I had the opportunity to be flexible with my time.

(**BTW**, that's an indication that I have an excellent doctor who actually takes her time with us.)

Guess who was there!!

My friend, Shawnna! Therefore, I sat with her for a few minutes during her treatment. Then went downstairs to chat with my navigator Elizabeth to show her the video from my last chemo...

Yep, I did all that, lol.

Well, my visit with Dr. K was good. It was really just a follow-up and an update on the status of my surgery. She wants to start me after surgery on some kinda pill which, **BTW**, I've already forgotten its name. But what I do know is that it can potentially increase my menopause symptoms, meaning if I think the hot flashes are bad now, this pill, in conjunction with the shot, gonna make me really sweat! (Oh Lord, I'm 'bout to pass out just thinking about it) Another side effect is achiness, but Elizabeth said it's nothing compared to the achiness from chemo. And there was one other side effect I can't think of right now related to menopause.

Man, life for the next couple of years will be an adjustment. And I'm glad I'm opening your eyes to see that treatment doesn't end at chemo. Technically, I'll still be on treatment for the next five-ten years on my insurance. Wow!

Oh! I remember telling her, "Remember I said I wanna have kids," so I'm not sure if the other side effect was related. But maybe so, cause if she said it was gonna make me menopausal, then I'm pretty sure that's it. Like, okay, I'm not gonna refuse treatment, but first, she told me five years now and an additional five years. Like **WTH**! I'll be 45! Mann, that's like saying that on my 45th birthday, we will be baby-making right away! Lol, seriously!!! Dang.

But hey! Like I said, Halle Berry and all them other starz did it. So can I! My main priority right now should be, being

NED (having no evidence of disease!) So like she said, we'll cross that bridge when the time comes. But five years. For sure, I'll be on both.

Lord, thank you for bringing me this far; thank you for my friends who encourage and uplift me, and Lord, thank you for my strength. You are the great I AM. Amen.

TUESDAY, JANUARY 16
Sleep. Sleep. Sleep!

One of the things Dr. K wants me to change is my sleeping pattern. Not only because she wants me to put Emil to bed at "Human Hours," lol:) But I'm pretty sure she said it for the health benefits as well.

For instance, working late at night can increase your risk of Breast Cancer.

I know, right?!? Like dang! All these risk factors. But yep.

I once saw an article that said women who work late at night have a higher risk of Breast Cancer.

Dr. K said there was a study done on it, and while it seemed true, there are sooo many other risk factors, such as having your period before eleven years old, giving birth after thirty... there's just a lot. But overall, having a healthy sleep pattern is good for all of us.

Man, it's gonna be a challenge cause I'm a night owl. I stayed up all night during my pregnancy; that's why the child can't sleep now! Lol, but I gotta do it.

So maybe I'll start by shutting down by 10 pm for starters. And go from there. Ugh, what a challenge!

FRIDAY, JANUARY 19
Grace

Morning.

Soon I'm gonna be asking for some home addresses, so get ready, **XOXO**.

Well, yesterday was a very productive day for me. I worked on some projects, took my baby to his appointment, exercised, started my daily devotional, and ended my day with Bible Study.

I feel so good to say it was a "productive day." Praise God that I have the strength to get up and go. That right there is a testimony. I just keep telling myself, "I'm healed, ain't no Cancer left within me," and as my pastor reminded me this morning, surgery will reveal "no residue or evidence of disease." I claim it in the name of Jesus!

Today I wanna share a real quick testimony of God's grace with y'all. I shared my diagnosis with the nurse yesterday at Emil's appointment. And she looked at me and said, "Have you been to the doctor for it yet?" And I said, "Yes, I just finished chemo, and I'm getting ready to have surgery." She just kept looking at me and said, "My niece had it, and you're gonna be just fine."

But then, what really made me think that perhaps she didn't hear the chemo part was when she said, "You have a port?!?!" Lol, as if she was in disbelief about me doing chemo. (I'm telling y'all, chemo is not what people think it is. At least not for everyone.)

Oh yeah, and I'm not sure if I told y'all, but even one of the receptionists at the center Monday thought I was talking about someone else when I was scheduling my "port flush." (A quick procedure I have done at the end of each treatment to avoid infection to the port).

Friends, it's nothing but the Grace of God, along with my attitude. I refuse to let Cancer control me. And I refuse to give up. God's been too good to me. Therefore, I know that He can and will heal me.

But please uplift me.

I won't lie; there are days the enemy tries to play tricks with my mind. (Having me believe I'm still leaking or experiencing pain from it.) But I know it's nothing but anxiety due to surgery, So I keep telling myself, "Evelina, you're gonna be alright...it's all gone" ...

Lord grant me peace in those hours

Thank you all for your prayers. By His stripes, we are all #Healed!

BTW, my hair is growing!!!

TUESDAY, JANUARY 23
A Darn Thing!

"I don't feel a darn thing!"

That's what Dr. C said to me today after my breast exam. A dramatic response!

What a relief it was to hear him say that, then what an overwhelming feeling it was when he presented me with several surgical options...

But after giving it some thought, we both decided that I'm having another MRI, mammo, and ultrasound done for peace of mind. Just to double-check, they've got everything. Of course, the tests aren't 100%, but they're as close to accurate as they can get. And for me, it's the best decision versus rushing to the surgery table just to get it over with.

So Warriors, please uplift me in prayer for **NEGATIVE** test results!!

I just want them to go in there, pinpoint the area, remove the port, stitch me up, and for it never to return in the name of Jesus.

So the 8th of February it is!

And I'm believing and declaring that everything will be alright.

Overall I've got to say it was a wonderful day.

Praise the Lord. Hooray!

WEDNESDAY, JANUARY 24
Trust You

Song of Inspiration: "Trust in You" by Anthony Brown and group therAPy.

Lord, as I prepare for this upcoming surgery, **I MUST** remind myself that you did not create me to worry.

Be Encouraged.

SATURDAY, JANUARY 27

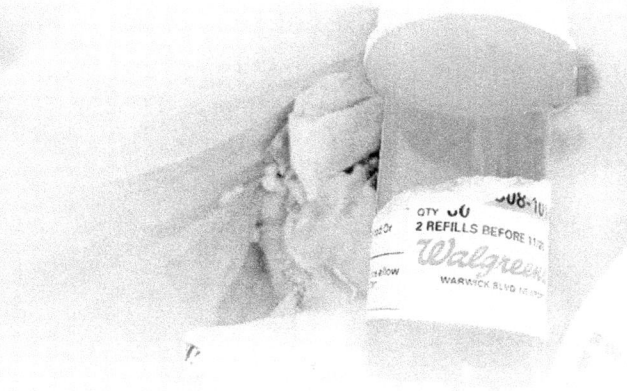

Aaaaand...in the trash you go!

Yay! No more steroids!! Praise God that part of my life is over. Dr. K had told me at my appt that I could get rid of them, and I thought I had, but last night, they went straight in the trash.

Aaaamen. No more 10 pm pills and waking up at 4 am. I'm done with all that.

Lord, you are good!

Oh, **BTW**, I forgot to tell y'all what Dr. C said to me, something like, "Sometimes the good Lord takes us through things."

And he's sooo right cause I'm a firm believer that everything happens for a reason. Sure, in the beginning, I broke down and told Dr. K, "I don't wanna be here," but as the days passed, I surrendered and allowed the Lord to use me.

Cause this right here was nothing for Him...it was just another test for me...and guess what?!? I passed it y'all!! I declare that I passed it!! Cause I'm confident that He's got me. And as always, He's gonna see me through.

In Jesus's name, Amen.

SUNDAY, JANUARY 28
Mammos oo

Not to scare anyone, but Breast Cancer can happen at any age.

Infact, I remember years ago watching a talk show about a little girl who was diagnosed at about 10 or 11 years old. Can you believe that?? (I bet it was The Maury Show before he switched to testing for baby daddies, lol)

Therefore, I encourage every woman with a suspicious lump or concern not to be afraid to talk to their physician. I believe the mammo age for most insurances is 40, and from my understanding, that's being raised again.

But we all know it shouldn't be denied to younger women, that's why so many of us have delayed stages. Heck! Even the doctors always wanna say, "oh, you're too young for anything!" Bump that! Write a referral!!! Rule it out!! Remove our doubts! But nope, sadly, for many of us, they won't listen till it's too late.

SMH. Life.

Thankfully, the good news is that my sisters will be able to get their yearly mammograms due to my diagnosis.

In fact, one of them just did last week, and it's **NEGATIVE**!!! Praise God.

So ladies, whether you have a concern or not, please stay on top of your check-ups. And If you do have a suspicion, please tell your physician. Don't be afraid, for some women don't even have to go through chemo! If that's your worst fear.

For, as they say, Early detection is the best prevention!

Love you all **XOXOXO**.

WEDNESDAY, JANUARY 31
The Unexpected

Buenas.

Hope everyone had a lovely morning. As for me, mannn, I started my day with three back-to-back appointments. Ugh!

And to think my surgery next week starts at 7 am. Nooooo (already dreading it).

Well, today, I had an MRI, mammo, and ultrasound. Various different scans to compare against the ones I had done six months ago.

AND WHAT DID THE DOCTOR SAY?!?

To be honest, when the diagnostic doctor walked in, I couldn't help but start crying... I swear it was like deja vu all over again. He said, "The good news is..." Then after that, I just kinda shut down cause if someone says that, it's usually followed by a bad report.

So after he left and I composed myself, I asked the tech, "Can you please repeat what he just said? Was it good news or bad news?" And she said, "he's saying he expected the area to be much larger than it is, but it's not, so that's good news!"

Lord, you are good!

Now the question still remains, how do we proceed? Do I continue with my lumpectomy and trust God that Dr. C will get it all? Or do I go for a partial mastectomy to remove any doubts in my mind?

No one else can make that decision but me. But the good news is the techs are pleased with my scans, and God surpassed their expectations.

Just like He always does. Amen.

Pray for me, friends. Xoxoxo.

#Healed

FRIDAY, FEBRUARY 2
Lumpectomy

Heyyy y'all.

Today, I met with Dr. C. He explained that because I had such a terrific response to chemo, they could no longer see where the tumor was. Yay!

The flip side is that this makes it hard for them to know exactly where to find a clear margin to cut around the Cancer.

Dear Lord, it's your supernatural power that shrunk an 8 to 10 cm area down to nothing, and it's in your power that we trust you'll guide the hands of the surgeon. In your son's name, we pray. Amen.

Looking forward to a successful lumpectomy.

breastCancer.org/treatment/surgery/lumpectomy

SUNDAY, FEBRUARY 4
What If..

Hey, y'all.

Woke up this morning around 3 or 4 am. sick. Ughhhh, I know that pizza from Chuck E Cheese's tore my stomach up!

You see, I'm already sensitive to tomato and then having most likely still some chemo in me made it worse. My body rejected aaaall of it, including the pills I was trying to take to ease the pain. **SMH**.

But I'm feeling a lil better now. Just hoping I don't have any more episodes.

Anyhow. Today's blog is titled "What If," and as much as I hate to entertain the idea, I wanted to school y'all a little bit.

What if??? Ugh! Well, if, for some reason, Dr. C and his team are unable to get clear margins, I have to be prepared to lose my right breast. I knoooow. I hate to even think about it. Mainly because I never thought I'd have to think about any "ifs" and that they would know exactly what to do if any issues arise.

But friends, just know that the ultimate goal is my life. Some people would say to eliminate any doubts, just cut it all off! But I know myself, and let's say I cut it off and later find out the Cancer is all gone. I would beat myself up for not trusting God the first go around, so I'm going this route first.

Sooo please just pray with me that everything will be alright. Deep down inside, I know it will be, but the technicalities of these things can drive someone crazy.

Yes, this is crazy. Wow!! That area is pretty much down to nothing! Dear Lord, I beg of thee. Please, if you've gone this far, guide the hands of Dr. C to make the right cut.

Blow our minds with no evidence of disease!!! In Your son's precious name. Amen.

THURSDAY, FEBRUARY 8
It Stings!!!!

Good morning; thank you for your prayers. I feel them. **XOXO**.

Just finished my first procedure of the day. Maaaan, it stung. A needle right into my areola. Omg. This shot is to help Dr. C identify any lymph nodes involved (sentinel Lymph node injection only with non-imaging). Look it up!

Two or three more to go at this center. Will keep y'all updated.

THURSDAY, FEBRUARY 8
The Stress

Hey y'all,

It's done! A successful lumpectomy was performed, and now the waiting game begins.

OMG, soooo after the injection, I had a wire localization. Where three thin wires were inserted into the biopsy sites. Sorry, y'all. I really wanted to take pictures, but it ended up being an emotional procedure.

A "talk" was given to me by Dr. P that should've been given to me the day I was diagnosed and not the day of surgery, and I was sooo overwhelmed.

Friends, why can't doctors just all have a round table talk together to come up with **ONE** agreeable game plan!!!

Dr. C shared good news last week, but I got Dr. P's expertise and concerns today. I was sooo emotional that he then called Dr. C so they could talk. But in the end, after another talk with me, Dr. C reminded me that "the good Lord is looking out for me." Oh yeah and I can't remember which one of them said it, but they said, "If I had to choose between trusting God or my doctor, I'd put my trust in **HIM**!"

Dear Lord, please give us the cure to this disease... please!!!

I just want more than a lil peace. I want the peace that surpasses Alllllllll understanding. I know they all want what's best for me. I just want everyone to be on the same page, so I can gain a greater understanding of it all. But ultimately, it's in your hands, dear Lord. Ultimately you have the final say. You are the one that can beat the statistics and clear every and any abnormal cell.

I trust you, Lord.

BTW, I'm cosmetically pleased :) Jesus, you are worthy to be praised.

FRIDAY, FEBRUARY 9

It's 7 am. And I'm up early thinking about everything the diagnostics doctor said.

And why do they just not allow the same doctor who biopsies you to be the one to give you the verdict.

Dr. P is concerned about my future and developing something else. Based on another angle and me being such a young woman.

All I can think about is the doctor who said, "It's just as effective to do this as that..."

Lord, help me. A part of me is saying just remove it and get a new one. So everyone will just leave me alone. Besides, for years, they never saw a problem with that breast when clearly something was wrong. It may not have been Cancer then, but something was "abnormal."

Removing it won't bother me, but why the expert opinion on the day of the procedure?

Lord, I just want peace and clarity. Embrace me.

I felt so drained yesterday with all that info. Here I am, rejoicing about the tumor disappearing when apparently, none of that seemed to matter.

Drained, **SMH**.

TUESDAY, FEBRUARY 13
The Call

Heyyy, everyone.

Looks like I'll be back under the knife!

Although Dr. C did a great job with my lumpectomy, there's still some small tumors found at the bottom left margin.

So now my options are to either remove more tissue or just say, "Just cut it! No more, "and in honesty, he said he'd feel safer cutting it. And in response, I agree. So next week, we're going back to the drawing board to talk. Ugh!

But it's okay. If it wasn't Cancer bothering my breast all these years, at least now someone is getting to the root of the problem for me. And what better team to help than the one I have now.

On another note…

Ain't it funny, I remember asking myself, "Will my faith still be as big if I faced a mastectomy??!?" And now, here I am today, facing one. I guess God must've said, "Well, let me put you to the test." Ain't that something?!?

WOW!

They're taking my "problem child away." Now I'm wondering what my new one will look like. Dear Lord, my prayer now is, please save my nipple.

Lol for real, tho! Leave me some kinda remembrance. Lol.

Pray for me, y'all. #surviva! #Healed

SUNDAY, FEBRUARY 18

Hi friends,

Thank y'all so much for checking on me. By now I would've been kept y'all posted, but I've been slacking. No excuses! **SMH**.

SOOO LINA, HOW YOU BEEN?!?

Well, I'm feeling much better, thank God, after being in the ER all afternoon Friday. Honestly, I don't know what happened that evening, but my arm was throbbing and swollen.

And obviously, it must've been of concern also to the doctor on call cause they ran a CT scan and performed some blood work.

GIIIIRL, YOU GOTTA TAKE IT EASY?!?

I knoow! SMH, I don't know what I was thinking, but the night before, I was collaborating with another artist on a project, then I decided to drive Friday cause I had an appt with Dr. K., Which **BTW** was rescheduled. But yep, apparently, my body wasn't ready for either activity. And the crazy thing is I thought I was still taking it easy, smh.

AND WHAT DID THE RESULTS SAY?!?

Praise God everything came out normal... The doctor said I just gotta take it easy and use a heating pad and then he prescribed me some different pain pills. (Did I tell y'all I'm not a fan of pills??... I avoid them at all cost)

Anyway, ughhhh. I'm so ready for this to be over. I'm dreading the thought of being under the knife again Loooord, nooo.

Pray for me, y'all.

And thank you, sis Uta, for driving me from one **ER** to the next. "Mam, you have seven people in front of you, and the first one has been waiting for three hours." Oooooh heck no! So off to Williamsburg we went.

And she knows I wouldn't have had her driving on a work night unless I was truly in pain. Xoxo.

Lord, please touch me. Please heal every part of my body. Yesterday I was having second thoughts about something. So please steer me the right way, knowing that in the end, you will get all the honor and all the glory for my complete and total restoration in Jesus's name. Amen

Love y'all.

TUESDAY, FEBRUARY 20
Monday

Well, friends, Monday it is.

Monday, Feb 26, is the day I'll say bye-bye to one of my girls for good. The problem child, the troublemaker, the one that for sooo long drove me crazy. And yes, the very same one that got me here. **SMH**.

Dear Lord, it was a difficult decision to say, "let's remove it." And yes, I know right now my life should be the overall focus and not a boob, but still, I can't help but think if the actions taken "yesterday" could've changed the outcome of my "today"?!?!

Ughhhhh. I don't wanna do this, pleeease.

Btw I'ma tell you now. Don't come at me talking bout, " Oh, they'll give you a new one," "Don't be so attached," "It's just a boob," this, this, and that. Cause right now, unless you know what it's like to lose a part of your body, I don't wanna hear it. Cause you can't possibly begin to process what I'm feeling. "She" was a part of my womanhood; I have every right to grieve and feel this way if I want to.

So forgive me if I take a moment to not be the super Christian that everyone perceives I am. But today wasn't easy.

Big deep breath

Moving on. With the power of our almighty God, the good news is chemo killed about 90% of the overall Cancer. And Dr. C says, "I choose to focus on the positive," and he's right. Amid my disappointments, I gotta thank God for that.

LINA, WHAT ABOUT HAVING ANOTHER LUMPECTOMY AGAIN???

Yeah, that was, again, another option. In fact, asking if another round or two of chemo would clear it up crossed my mind. But given the history of this "chick," in addition to the pathology report (which I ripped into pieces at the office), I don't want to prolong my treatments anymore.

Not to say that I don't trust God by keeping "her," but everyone's individual case is different, and I've gotta discern and hear His voice through the mouths of the ones He's placed my health in...

I mean, let's be real. No one wants to be under the microscope every second of their lives. No one! And certainly not me. So that's another reason why I choose to trust my "dream team."

And I'm sorry, y'all. I don't mean to rant. But maybe God is using me furthermore so that y'all can see that the battle ain't over at chemo, heck! For many women, chemo is followed by surgery after surgery, radiation, reconstruction, shots, chemo pills, more chemo, preventative pills, and whatever else, depending on their treatment.

Maaannnn, that's a lot!. Heck yeah! Tell me about it. **SMH**.

Dear Loooord, please give me the strength I need to endure the test!!! I tried my best to keep "her," I was rooting for this "chick" all along. I had faith in this "chick." I admit I must give her credit cause "she" did fight the good fight. But now, after 35 years, she's retiring and leaving me. Nooo.

SMH. Lord, you must truly think I'm a warrior with all I've been through?! Huh??

P.S. By the way, my "save the nipple" campaign....it ain't happening. I know, great idea, but in my case, since I'm not having immediate reconstruction, it's best to reconstruct that as well. Well daaamnnn. Just take that away from me too?!? Lol.

Y'all know what that means. Evelina will be taking a pic of every single detail of this "chick" before they chop "her" off. Cause whoever this plastic surgeon is, he/she is gonna get it right the first time. I'm an artist. And yes, I expect you, doctor, to be able to turn my vision into reality!

Keep the prayers coming.

Love, Lina.

THURSDAY, FEBRUARY 22
Existence

Morning.

As I prepare for my appointment with Dr. K. I can't help but think about my devotional this morning. From a new book I'm reading called "I Declare, 31 Promises To Speak Over Your Life." Day one today talks about being careful with our words because life and death, as we know, lie in the power of our tongues.

Well, with that being said, this post may seem a lil shocking to y'all, but in a way, now that I kick back and think about things. What is happening in my today was prophesied in my yesterday.

BUT HOW LINA?? YOU DIDN'T DO ANYTHING WRONG!

I know. And this post is not to blame myself, but I remembered being at a doctor's visit just this morning. The **OBGYN** knew I'd been back and forth with that breast. He joked and said something like, "are we gonna have to cut that breast?" And we both laughed a lil cause I mean, I had been back and forth with the nipple leaking. So I understood exactly what he was saying. Cause sometimes, I used to have one finger that itched me so bad every now and then, and those same thoughts would cross my mind.

And ohhh, remember another instance when I looked at

myself in the mirror years ago, placed my hand over that breast and thought to myself, "Is this how I would look without it??"

I knoooow...it sounds crazy...but yeah, when "she" gave me trouble and the doctors kept saying there was nothing, those thoughts crossed my mind.

Instead of thoughts like "I'm going to get better," "I'ma keep pushing for a solution," "Cancer will not be a visitor in my body," and "Every cell in my body is functioning right." Then maybe this chapter of my life would've been different.

So my word of encouragement for you today is to speak life. In every situation, speak life. Don't talk bad about yourself. Throw out those old thoughts and begin to see yourself as healthy, stable, and renewed. So that the words you speak today don't take root in your tomorrow.

Love y'all

"... be transformed by the renewing of your mind...."
Romans 12:2 NIV

FRIDAY, FEBRUARY 23
The Impossible

Hey friends, how are ya?

Today has been an okay day. Had to make a few calls and even spoke with Dr. C because my surgery is now being rescheduled to April 9th. That way, we can decide the best way to go about my reconstruction. So between now and then, I'll be meeting the plastic surgeon and my radiologist.

Ughh, this still feels sooo unreal.

In fact, I thought for a second, "Maybe, God's gonna take this opportunity to give me an explosive blessing. To do the impossible. To give me a miracle, to show me that He can take that 10% left and make it alllll disappear with no treatments whatsoever."

Sounds crazy, huh? I know, but that's what you call "crazy faith." Cause I've heard some wild testimonies about those who were healed with just the power of Prayer or the touch of the Holy Spirit, leaving doctors wondering, "What the heck?!"

In fact, yesterday, as Dr. K was talking to me, she said something like, "I know you prayed and had faith and this and that. But you gotta make lemonades with the lemons you've been given." I'm pretty sure she wasn't tryna tell me prayer didn't work, it failed, or anything negative. But in my mind, for some reason, the enemy tricked me into believing that she was tryna imply that "Your God failed you."

But Devil, you're a liar because, just as Joel Osteen said, "I don't care what the medical report says, you are the child of God, and you will be **HEALED**. Maybe not the way you imagined, but it shall come true!"

And just now, I had to tell myself, "Evelina, you know that!!!! You know the good Lord got you, just like Dr. C always says."

So friends, in the weeks ahead, as I meditate on His word and speak healing into my body, pray for me. Pray, that I may be patient as God does the impossible, whatever that may be.

Cause although both doctors have agreed that removing it now is what's best for me, based on the report. Dr. C, for some reason, keeps telling me, "but once I cut it off, I can't put it back on," and that right there, for some reason, makes me wanna "give the lumpectomy another chance."

Ughhhh. I hate being in a state of confusion. Lord, help me!!!

Please help me relax my mind and speak to my body. Please do the impossible. Please reveal to them "no evidence of disease." Touch me, Jesus, please. From the top of my head to the tip of my toes, touch me, please. I command my body to heal. I command every single cell to function right. I command all these things in the only name that's more powerful than any other name. Your son Jesus, Amen.

Healing Prayer

Dear God,
Your Words are HEALTH.
I ask for physical healing.
I speak to my body
...your energy
...your abundance
...your comfort
...your clarity.
NOTHING IS IMPOSSIBLE to you.
You are God of an abundant life.
I claim that life now.
I think of an activity which is a stretch for me.
I hold a vision of myself carrying out this
activity with EASE.
I see myself
I celebrate this health improvement.
Thank you, God.
Amen.

HEALINGCFSME.COM

SUNDAY, FEBRUARY 25
Bullets

*"To see a **bullet** or **bullets** in your dream indicate anger and aggression directed at you or someone else. You need to be cautious on what you say and do. Your actions and words may easily be misinterpreted. To **dream** of being hit by a **bullet** suggests that you need to persevere and endure the difficult times."* dreammoods.com

Wow! My dreams always seem to speak to me.

TUESDAY, MARCH 6
#Surviving

Hey friends, sorry I'm slacking.

Since my last entry, I've been healing pretty well. In fact, I just wish that this was it for me some days. Not only so I can keep it moving but because my scars look sooo darn good. Dr. C did an amazing job. And I just pray the mastectomy scar heals just as faintly. Ughhhh more surgeries. Nooooooo.

On the flip side, Guess what?? I got my eyebrows waxed!!! Can you believe I finally had enough hair to get them done since August, when I last did them? Wow! I was lying there thinking, "I can't believe this is happening." I was very excited cause them suckas grew overnight. Honestly, I hadn't paid much attention when my eyelashes and eyebrows fell off. But God is good cause just as fast as chemo took 'em away. He gave them back to me and in abundance!! Lol.

But yeah, they grew back, and so did the rest of the hairs on my body. In fact, I even shaved my legs yesterday! And most importantly, I can slick down the hair on my head. **BTW**, the short look is growing on me. The only thing that isn't is all the gray strands I can't seem to pluck out.

BTW, please pray for my upcoming lab work. I'm not sure if it's my sleeping pattern or too much screen time on the computer, but at times I feel dizzy. So my doctor's gonna check on a few things for me. He thinks it could be a chemo side effect, but I need to know for sure. (Thank you, Father, in advance for healing my body.)

In the meantime, I'm healing wonderfully, working, driving, and surviving like a true warrior. I trust God, and I know that I'm already healed in the name of Jesus.

Love y'all. XOXO.

TUESDAY, MARCH 13
Loving Me

Hey, y'all...how's everyone on this beautiful day. I haven't posted on a regular because, honestly, I've been trying to forget about the battle. I just wish I was all done, and this would all be behind me.

But just now, after hearing my mother cry because a friend of hers just passed away from Melanoma Cancer, I said to myself I must post something.

Well, over the days, I've been embracing the new me. My hair is growing like crazy, and yesterday I told someone, "I'm feeling sexy." The style is growing on me, and the best part is I don't even need a man to tell me I look good for me to feel sexy with my short do. (Hello!)

On another note, there are days I feel slightly guilty about my health. Hearing people say things like, "I'm tryna stay healthy, healthy this, healthy that," makes me feel like I should've done the best I could to stay healthy. But like I was discussing with a friend of mine, even the healthiest person can be walking around with Cancer in their body without even knowing it. And that's scary! So instead of feeling guilty or uncomfortable around such statements, I should tell myself, "My God is just using me," which is true!

In my opinion, my God is just using me to encourage someone in my shoes to testify to His goodness, to declare His healing power. What happened to me can happen to anyone, but the good news is, "My story is not your story, and yours is not mine." God uses each of us in different ways, and just because He's decided to use me this way doesn't mean that it'll happen to you.

Stay on top of your checkups!

Love y'all. Xoxo.

THURSDAY, MARCH 15
Heartbreak

I just found out today that one of my sister's **BFF** has Stomach Cancer. Such heartbreaking news. But how many of you know that we serve a healer! The doctor, above all doctors!

I know a lady who beat that very same Cancer more than once and was even resuscitated multiple times on what was meant to be her deathbed. But God!

I'm telling you, there is nothing too hard for our God. And I believe and declare that she's also healed in the mighty name of Jesus.

God's got you, girl! Xoxoxo.

Side note, my letter of encouragement to my sister:

Thinking of your friend today. My first appointment wasn't easy; I bawled. But as I bawled, thinking of everything negative, my ears were closed to the good news God was delivering to me even in the midst of the storm. But as humans, it's natural to have those feelings but remember that God still heals today as He did way back then. Stay positive, have faith, and know who's the Dr. Above all, Doctors. And declare, "But My

God says..." and begin to command every single cell to function back in order! Despite the prognosis.

#Healed

MONDAY, MARCH 19

Radiation

Hey, y'all. Just coming back from meeting my radiologist, Dr. L.

And as of today, my treatments with him will start on April 30th!!! Whoo-hoo. Mann, I can't wait to get started and get this over with. (Enough time for me to be healed after surgery)

He predicts it'll be about five to six weeks for 30 minutes daily. And he feels that based on my response to chemo, I shouldn't have any problems with side effects. Besides the skin tanning a lil, the good news is it doesn't stay that way forever "if" it happens at all. And I may get a Lil fatigued, but it's nothing compared to what I felt with chemo.

What I thought was cool was I'll be getting my first tattoo :) . Lol, it's just two small dots that will indicate to the machine exactly where to treat me. Pretty neat, huh?

SO TELL US, YOU LIKE YOUR NEW DR. LINA?

Yeessss. He's a lovely man, but at first, when he was talking to me, I started tearing up. I don't know why, but I felt like he was nervous or something, as if I was gonna refuse treatment. I didn't know what it was. So I asked him, "Are you scared for me? Cause I know, I'ma be Cancer-free. I know this is gonna work!" And he said, "No, I'm not scared for you." And later, after speaking to my navigator, she tells me he's just a very soft-spoken man. Bless his heart. It was strange cause I'm so used to Dr. K being a lil hyper at times, lol. And Dr. C, who's just sooo positive about everything.

But other than that, Dr. L is a lovely man (Another top doc!). I look forward to God using him to treat the remaining cells. By the way, he mentioned about 99% of it is gone. And the radiation is to prevent the tumor from growing back again and to treat the lymph nodes being that my test came out positive.

But God is good cause I know He's got me. This mess ain't coming back, and every single cell in the name of Jesus will function back in order.

Love y'all. **XOXOXO**.

P.S. Tomorrow, I see Dr. G for my blood work results. Prayers up!

TUESDAY, MARCH 20
Flashback

Good morning y'all! 'Bout to get up and do some work

before heading to my appointment and before this lil boy wakes up.

But yesterday, I kept thinking about my trip to the ER about a month ago or so. When the doctor asked me if I had any medical problems, I said something like "none other than "just the Cancer." And he chuckled and said, "I like how you said that. **JUST** 'the' Cancer."

I mean, I know what he was tryna say, that I'm saying it as if it's not **THAT BIG** of a deal, but how else am I supposed to say it?? I'm not gonna be sitting here crying about it all the time or making other people feel sorry for me because I have Cancer. What good is that?? I gotta pick my head up high and not let that "word" phase me. Cause I'ma beat this thing! God's got this thing! I'm already Cancer-free in the name of Jesus.

But I understand this flashback was also to help me understand that this ain't nothing to be taken lightly. That's why Dr. L speaks the way he does. Cause this is a serious matter (not saying the others don't take it seriously). I should've told him yesterday, "save the speech, just sign me up!... Dr. K already told me I can't refuse anything...and besides, I wasn't refusing a darn thing anyway" Ssssshhhht whatever they gotta do, just do it. Like my mom said, I'm over the worst, chemo.

XOXO. Thank you all for listening to me. I'm sooo grateful for your support and words of encouragement. Until my next blog, Lina.

MONDAY, MARCH 26
Rooted

Morning y'all. Ugh, it's eeeearly, smh, and I'm not a morning person at all.

Well, tomorrow, I see Dr. K and Dr. C for a follow-up. And **BTW**, my appointment with Dr. H went pretty well. But I'll elaborate more on it once I see Dr. C cause I wanna make sure we're all on the same page before I tell y'all my decision.

But overall, he's pretty down to earth, and ironically, he used to live out in Georgetown, close to Rosslyn Metro station. Which is exactly where I attended college, The Art Institute of Washington. What a coincidence, huh?

Well, today, I'd like to talk about being rooted.

Throughout this journey, I'd sometimes say, "I wonder if my faith is strong because I'm not facing a mastectomy? Because surely if I was, I'd be a mess." And now here I am, about two weeks away from losing my right breast. Smh.

But you know what? Thank God that I can say that after the shock, after the tears, after the pain, after the disappointment, my faith is still rooted in God!

My testimony all along has been I'm healed! I'm **HEALED**! Not, I'm healed, and I kept my breast. But I'm **HEALED**. I'm Cancer-free! The Lord Saved me! I'm alive! I'm well!

Surely I wanted to save my breast, but the most important thing to me must be my life. Therefore I must still fight and know that even though I have to face the unexpected, God's promise still stands. I'm **HEALED**.

Amen.

SATURDAY, MARCH 31
Don't Worry

Hey, y'all.

The countdown begins. Monday, April 9th, it is. I'll be having a right breast mastectomy and an expander placed to start the reconstruction process. Then, my doctors will come together to come up with a timeline.

Let me tell y'all, if there's one thing I don't like about this whole thing, it's the doctor visits. I mean, I've got a doctor for everything, then I'm left to make all these decisions, which I understand. Yes, it's my body. But sometimes I'd rather them just tell me, "Okay, Evelina, we're gonna do this, this, that, and here's the action plan outlined," cause sometimes I feel overwhelmed and out of it. I be like, "Dear Lord!!!! I just want to see the end of the tunnel."

Well, anyhow, I saw Dr. K, and after surgery, we hope to be starting my preventative pills. (Praising God in advance that all goes well with the approval.) I also saw Dr. C; I'm telling y'all he should be a minister because he always encourages me.

For instance, I told him I was nervous about my lymph nodes during my appointment. And he said, "I didn't tell you I'm taking any more out. And the good Lord tells us not to be worried about things we shouldn't be worried about. I'm betting you're gonna live!" I told him, "I have no doubts about making it, but sometimes worry kicks in." And again, he said to me, "We'll tell you when to worry, and right now, you have nothing to be worrying about." He's such an angel, and I wish all doctors were like him.

With that being said, my word of encouragement for y'all tonight is, "Don't worry. The good Lord tells us not to worry, and you, my dear, have nothing to be worried about." Thanks, Dr. C!

Love y'all. xoxoxo.

SUNDAY, APRIL 1
What's Up???!

Lol, I'm laughing cause it feels like when I don't post regularly, I've got a waterfall of words just waiting to come out. Lol. So forgive me, y'all!.

This blog is titled What's up cause many of you have been asking what I've been up to. So here's a lil recap of the highlights in my life.

Yesterday I attended The first Saturday Reach Experience at Gethsemane Baptist Church. A non-traditional Saturday service for those who cannot make it to church on Sunday. Hosted by the anointed Riddicks! It was powerful, and my guests loved it!

Next...

I had an awesome time at the 8th Walk In It Inc. Women's Conference. **OMG!** Like I tell everyone, I never really used to believe in prophecy till I experienced it. Which is funny because I believed in fortune tellers but not in the anointing. (Crazy, huh?!?) But anyhow, when one of the speakers prayed for me, I couldn't help but start crying. Because everything the Holy Spirit revealed to her about me was on point! And the funny thing is I've never even met this woman before! But she said, "God is saying don't be afraid to speak. Sometimes you scare yourself when you speak. But continue speaking."

This is sooo true because I truly believe in the power of spoken words. And as I've shared with y'all before, my business! My Honda! Rising from the wheelchair! My sailor in white! These are all spoken words, but sometimes I doubt my gift and am afraid to "speak." So God is reminding me, "Evelina, speak out your desires in confidence." Maaaannnn, what an amazing conference. Thanks, Rev. J!

Next...

I woke up one day last week with a nosebleed. Scared me cause it wasn't until the Taxol that I started experiencing that. But thank God my platelets came out good, and I just pray that it never happens again. Although I've heard that some side effects stay in you for a lil bit. But Dr. K thinks that's not my case, and it's just all related to it being nosebleed season.

Yep! So that's what's up.

BTW, Happy Easter, beautiful people!!! I forgot to tell y'all I'm part of the sermon this morning!!! I'm excited and nervous at the same time. But I pray that my testimony inspires somebody today. Pray for me, y'all.

SUNDAY, APRIL 1
It Ain't Over

Song of Inspiration: "It Ain't Over" by Norman C. Brown

Friends, it ain't over until God says it's over!

SUNDAY, APRIL 8
I'm Human

*"This is the day that the Lord has made.
I shall rejoice and be glad in it!"*

This Is the Day That the Lord Has Made,
Song by Listener Kids

Woke up this morning with this song on my heart. So I take it as a reminder that no matter what I'm going through, I must continue to rejoice every day for seeing "A New Day."

Loooord, just one more day. Just one more day, y'all. Man, I've been trying my best not to dwell so much on tomorrow, but I can't lie; some days, I feel like I'm about to break down and cry. I hate that this is happening, and every day I'm in the car alone, I find myself crying. Because the truth is I can't always be strong.

Yes, I'm also human y'all! I have feelings too! At times, it may seem like I'm superwoman through all this, but I have my breaking points too.

Imagine being told that you'll be losing a body part. Would you not cry? Would you not feel some type of way? Would you not take some time alone to let it sink in? This ain't easy, y'all. This ain't easy!!! Although I've heard many women say, "Just take them!" "They tried to kill me, take 'em," but the truth is, even those ladies mourn their loss too.

Dear Father, I know everything's gonna be alright; I feel your warm embrace as well. But please continue holding me the nights I'm alone during the healing process. Please remind me that I'll be okay. And that it won't be long till it's all over and done with. Cause I need you, I need you more and more each day.

I'm praying everything will expand well and that radiation will work out. As a matter of fact, I'm claiming it'll work. I'm claiming my skin will expand well, and the reconstruction will have no complications. I'm claiming that they will find no more abnormal cells or evidence of Cancer. I'm claiming the victory. I'm claiming that you have already healed me 100. I'm claiming it because I know your word and your promises never fail. So, Lord, I leave this surgery in your hands; I place both Dr. C and Dr. H in your care. I believe you have strategically placed each one of them in my life for a reason. And I believe I'm in the absolute best care. Cause it's in your son's name that I believe this. Amen.

Love, Lina.

SUNDAY, APRIL 8
That's powerful!

In conversation with my church sister, I said," My doctor is fighting to give me the best care." And she then looks at me and with very few words, she points upward. That's #powerful!

"Jesus is the great physician"
Unknown

SUNDAY, APRIL 8
The Big Day

My surgery is tomorrow, April 9th at 7:20 am. I have to be at the hospital, Riverside Pavilion Newport News, by 5 am. Ughhhh, I'm dreading it. But I'll be spending the night and staying for a 23-hour watch. (Looking forward to that hospital food, lol.) Pray for me, y'all.

Xoxoxo. **#Healed**.

SUNDAY, APRIL 8
When...

"When life gives you a hundred reasons to break down and cry, show life that you have a thousand reasons to smile and laugh. Stay strong."
unknown

SUNDAY, APRIL 8
Speak

Song of Inspiration: "Speak" by Jamar Jones / Johnnie W Jr. Murray

Remember that life and death lie in the power of our tongues. **SO SPEAK!** I continue to speak **HEALING**; what do you speak?

Be Encouraged.

MONDAY, APRIL 9
I'm Aight

Hey, y'all!

Thank you so much for the calls, texts, words of encouragement... prayers. And for following me.

You all are the best. And I'm so grateful to have each of you in my corner during this season of my life, sooo I got here this morning at 5 am. I was number one y'all! The first patient at the hospital, that was rare cause I'm hardly ever punctual. Lol, I was even here before the admin! Imagine that.

But anyway, they got me checked in around 5:30 am or so, I guess, and as I layed in the bed, I just kept taking pictures of my breast and tryna to document some things to share with y'all. For example, the vein machine. Have any of you ever heard of it? This machine was sooo freaking cool! All the nurse does is shine a light on my arm, and she can find every single vein in my body. It even shows her any recent bruises from previous blood draws. That way, she's careful not to poke me in the same area.

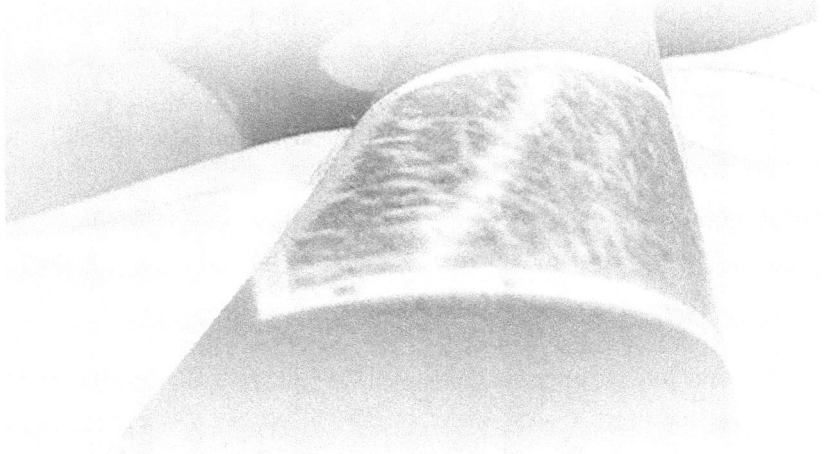

Next, after prep, the chaplain came in to pray with me. He was so nice and you know me, we chatted for a while. He shared how he's from Jamaica, has been in the **NAVY** and has even visited the Panama Canal! Great guy, and as we chatted, I also shared with him my writing and the prayer I had written yesterday. He was so encouraged that he'll be following my blog! That right there really touched me.

Next, my surgeons came in to show off their drawing skills. It was funny cause one of the nurses said, "Dr. C drew on you, but Dr. H is **REALLY** gonna draw on ya" Lol. So I told him, "I heard you graduated from the Art institute too, huh?!" Lol...I really looked like a drawing board.

I love my doctors, and Dr. C was in tears over the entry I wrote about him. He said, "Don't you ever forget that! So take that backpack off (in regards to my blog titled 'Don't Worry')."

After that, the nurse injected me, and the last thing I remembered was Dr. H holding my hand as I fell asleep. (Now, isn't that a beautiful memory?)

God, you are so good; thank you for these men in my life. They mean so much to me.

And now, here I am in the recovery room after a three-hour lengthy procedure. Tryna keep it together with pain meds and doing my best to nourish myself Smh, I boasted so much about eating it, but I don't have **THAT** appetite. As a matter of fact, I just threw all of it up. And if I do it again, I may have to stay here another night. So please pray for me, y'all.

But anyhow, overall, I'm doing good y'all. The only slight complication I had was maintaining enough oxygen straight after surgery. So for a couple hours, I had to stay hooked up to the breathing machine. But Praise God, for He's good! I'm here and I'm alive. Hallelujah!

Again, thanks for the prayers and I promise to keep y'all updated.

Hugs and kisses, Lina.

TUESDAY, APRIL 10

Not Bad

Hey, y'all!

Mannn, I'm so upset. I had like five paragraphs written, and since the reception sucks here, I lost it all while trying to post earlier. Nooooooo

Now here I am praying that it'll post successfully this time. I mean, I love writing, but dang, that's five paragraphs I gotta remember. Lol.

Anyhow, Dr. H gave me the option to stay another day. And one of my God mommies suggested I should do it being that Emil has a 24-hour bug. My thoughts, I'm taking it! For I need this extra time to rest and not risk any additional problems.

So pretty much all day, I've been resting and praising God that my appetite did pick up today by lunchtime. So I was able to enjoy a BBQ sandwich and then a turkey platter for dinner. Which, **BTW**, stayed in my stomach! Praise God, cause maaaan, I swear like every piece of that grilled chicken last night came out of me. But like Dr. H said, at times, that does happen after surgery with a mixture of the meds. Boiii, it was rough, y'all.

But anyhow. Guess what??!? I'm so proud of myself, friends. Today I was able to wash up and do my hair with little to no help. Of course, my arms bothered me a bit afterward, but overall the pain was tolerable.

In fact, I even had the strength mentally to look at myself. And it doesn't look bad at all! I swear I was nervous and thought it would take me some time to do it. But thank God for helping me face my fear. And I'm pretty sure having the expander in place helps me visualize my new breast versus having just a flat area.

Overall, it's been a good day. Thank you for your prayers. I'll be going home tomorrow for sure. After my breakfast meal, lol. Hey, I gotta enjoy one good hospital meal before I go.

Prayers up. Love y'all. Xoxoxo.

WEDNESDAY, APRIL 11
In the Middle

Good moooorning.

Just finished listening to Joyce Meyers this morning and her message for today was, "Don't give up in the middle."

And that really hit home because, after the lumpectomy, I did my best to stay strong-minded. Cause, like Pastor O'Donnell, just said, when you allow your soul to remain broken, that gives the enemy the perfect opportunity to take control.

So praise God for the strength He gives me day by day to smile in the midst of my trials. Thank God for the strength to go on, thank God that I'm not sitting around feeling sorry for myself, thank God for reminding me that joy cometh in the morning and thank God that "I know" that I'm only being used for His glory.

Yes! Father. Thank you for not allowing me to give up in the middle. Cause I could've easily turned on you when the report came back with a positive margin, or when the chemo would drain me, or even right now after losing a breast. Loooord, thank you for keeping me afloat and for not letting me give up in the middle.

Amen.

WEDNESDAY, APRIL 11
Home Sweet Home

Hey, y'all. Yes! I'm home now!!

Thank you sooo much for checking up on me. I think I made it home around 1 something or so. Just after my lunch meal. Which, by the way, was a grilled chicken sandwich. Yum-meee!

It was funny cause I got up this morning, sponged myself, did my hair, walked a lil, and started gathering my things. When Dr. H came by this morning, he said something like, "Man, look at you! You ready!" Lmbo. It was funny. And he's right; all I needed were the discharge papers cause I was ready to **GO**!

I said to him, "I'm glad I stayed an extra night cause I needed the rest. But I don't wanna get too used to being in bed; I have to motivate myself," and he said, "You're right, but some days will be better than others."

But guess what he told us today y'all?!? Dr. H is Panamanian! What in the world?!? So not only did he live in the same area I went to college in, but he's also Panamanian like me! Wow, it's definitely a small world for sure.

MY SURGEON. Handsome has a beautiful smile and is passionate about his field. Oh, and most importantly, he's a man of God. Speaking of that, did I tell y'all he'll be the guest speaker at this year's Pink Perseverance Dinner??

"It's going to be ok! Close those eyes.
Stop that mind. Say your prayers.
Sleep peacefully! God is working on your behalf!"
unknown

THURSDAY, APRIL 12

Tears

As much as I hate to think about it, this diagnosis affects not only me but those around me.

Heike Johnson
Apr 9 at 06:54

GM .. If y'all can please say a little prayer for my sister and for the surgeons that will be performing on her body this morning at 7...she's a little nervous and emotional about getting that troubled breast removed but my sister is soo strong but her faith in God is even stronger that she knows this right here will definitely KICK that CANCER out of her body!!!! Since August when we found out she was diagnosed with cancer I've seen my sister go through soo much but you wouldn't know it nor know she's battling this...I admire her strength and faith soo much..

> "In a very real way, the whole family has Cancer. Traditionally, we thought of the disease being contained within the patient. But if we look at it from the other lens, we see how it hits the emotions and social relationships of families."
> — Jason Carrol

> "When someone has Cancer, the whole family and everyone who loves them does, too."
> — Terri Clark

These quotes are nothing but the truth.

FRIDAY, APRIL 13
Popping

Lol. I've been popping them pills!!!

Ohh, lordy, yes, I have! Thanks to them, I could stand up for a wash-up (with my mom's help) and fellowship with my family in the living room.

Hmm. If I had to describe the pain I'm feeling, I'd say it's as if I have a silverware plate glued to the right side of my chest. And it's mainly the edges of that "plate" that bothers me once the meds start wearing off. (That's the best way I can describe it.)

And next time I see Dr. H, I'll take a picture of both the expander and silicone used for the reconstruction. Oh, and **BTW**, he said that my best reconstruction option is a tattooed nipple. As much as saving the nipple was a good idea to me, by the time I saw him, I never really stressed the idea or discussed nipple options. I guess I just thought he could make them, but he said something like the amount of tissue used to create a nipple would eventually shrink to at least 50% in the future, so a tattoo would probably be my best cosmetic choice.

It's incredible what these artists can do to make so many Cancer survivors like myself feel whole again.

Well, it's about time to pop another one. Lol. Thank y'all so much for checking on me. Each day gets a lil better. Xoxoxo.

Love Lina.

FRIDAY, APRIL 13
JP Drains

Oh my! How could I forget to mention the drains!?! As part of my home care, I'm responsible for emptying the two drains Dr. H placed on my right side to drain any excess fluid in that area.

Google it! JP Drains.

SATURDAY, APRIL 14
A Reason and A Season

It's 3:41 am, and Nurse "Mommy" has just finished helping me empty out one of my drains and administering my pain pill.

This sucks; the waiting period between taking the pill and when it kicks in sucks. I've always remembered Percocet as an instant pill, but this ain't no instant thing!

What the heck! Maaaann, it seems like it's taking forever. And while I'm waiting, I'm careful not only to breathe a certain way but to not move so much so that I can tolerate the pain. BTW it's not excruciating, but it's painful. As if something is pressing tightly against my chest wall. But anyhow, I just wanted to take a few minutes to talk about one of my dear followers. Mrs. Kelly W.

Mrs. Kelly and I met at a season in my life when I thought God had forgotten me. Just about two years ago, when I was pregnant and chasing after something God clearly didn't want for me. At least not in that season! Cause I believe, and I've been told, God's got something else planned beyond LinaImaging. In fact, I get nervous just thinking about it cause growing up, I've always been scared of public speaking. But many say that my testimony will stand before numerous crowds. (Chills.)

BTW, let me pause for a second to say that while writing that paragraph, I had to stop and walk back and forth in my room, exercising that arm to relax a tensed muscle. Wow! **OMG**, I swear it felt like somehow my chest was caving in. But now, after an hour's pause, my mom has rearranged my pillows, and this warm heating pad has me dozing off.

Come on now!!! Don't do this to me, Percocet!!!! I've got a good word for the people!!! Lol (sucking my teeth). Ugh.

Sorry, y'all. I've gotta make this part one of two.

Love y'all.

MONDAY, APRIL 16

A Reason and A Season P2

Take two! I'm sorry y'all about the other night, them Percocets **KNOCKED** me **OUT**! Lol.

But anyhow, Mrs. Kelly was, in fact, one of my assignment managers when I worked for a lil bit as a temp. And I've titled this blog as such because everything that happens in our lives is not meant to last us forever.

Yes, it's true. There are times when God allows us to meet certain people, go through particular situations, or be a part of an organization or group only for a reason or a season.

You see after working with the company for some time, I honestly thought, "This has got to be it! Surely this is the job God has for me, cause I ain't tryna be no business owner, oooh no! LinaImaging is not where I need to be!"

And after so many unsuccessful interviews and the depression from not having a guaranteed paycheck, it was easy for me to believe that God was answering a prayer for me.

And by a show of the "love button," how many of you can relate to thinking back to the times when you thought you had God's plan all figured out? Only to realize later that the way you envisioned things happening ended up taking on a whole 'nother direction cause, in fact, what He had for you was something far greater.

Well, that's precisely what happened to me. I thought I had God's plan aaaallll figured out. Friendly people, family-oriented, great benefits, beautiful location, free luncheons. Never mind that it wasn't my industry. I just honestly thought, "Lord, week after week, she's calling me, so surely this is what you have for me!" But when week after week came and there was no talk of hiring, I began to wonder, "Lord, why have you forgotten me?"

Boi, oh boi. Lol. I just gotta laugh every time I think about how strategic He is. You see, not long after working there, I ended up pregnant with Emil, and what's amazing about that situation is I would've never been qualified for health insurance with **PAID** maternity leave if **IT HAD NOT BEEN** for **THAT PARTICULAR ASSIGNMENT.**

A temp agency with **PAID** maternity leave??? Yes! Even my agent was like, "What in the world!!! Mrs. Johnson, you're so smart cause in all my years here, I've never known this one to be in the books!" But that's just like God! Always watching over us.

He's sooooo strategic. He's soooo amazing. He's sooooo powerful. He's sooooo perfect. He's God!

And let me tell you. I ended up staying with Mrs. Kelly until the end of my pregnancy. They loved me so much that they surprised me on my birthday, allowed me to make my own schedule, gave me a mini baby shower, and treated me as one of their own. I was positioned by God with the right people to bless me in the right season.

Forever grateful.

MONDAY, APRIL 16

Today

Hey, y'all.

Today, my sister Uta and baby Emil took me to my appointments. And guess who's back?!?

Ashleyyyy!!!!! She gave me my shot today and showed me all the beautiful pictures of Kenna.

But let me tell ya, I was concentrating so much on the mastectomy pain that my mentality was to hurry up, get that shot, and get out. Cause no matter whether I stood up or sat down, the pain in my body remained.

Anyways...

Sooooo I got my Lupron shot today. Praise God. Finally! But you know what's crazy? The exact spot where the needle is administered is right where I'm numb from the car accident; therefore, guess what??! I don't feel a darn thing! Not even a flinch. What a blessing! Cause I'm telling yall, that shot goes deeeeeeep down into the muscle. Right?! Ouch!

Thennnnn...

After that, we walked to my appt next door with Dr. H, and everything was healing perfectly as expected. He was able to pull one of my drains out (it burns a lil but otherwise not painful), and due to some constipation and concerns of mine, he was also able to change my medications so that I wouldn't be so drowsy all the time.

Just one more surgery, y'all and I'll be done.!!!! Then, as recommended, I'll swap out the silicone every couple of years for a new one, a preventative to any potential accidents. Although what's interesting is that he's created a "pocket" in my breast. So let's say heaven forbid if something was to happen to it, the fluid would be contained within that "pocket" versus traveling through my body. Isn't science amazing??!? Wow!

Once again, thank you all so much for checking on me and for your words of encouragement each day. God is good! And each day, my strength is renewed. Amen to that! Love y'all. Muah.

MONDAY, APRIL 16
My 80 Percent

I am in aweeee with the outpour of love. I'm lining up all my cards to motivate me each and every day.

Like Dr. K said, you all are my 80%. Your support definitely contributes to my healing.

WEDNESDAY, APRIL 18
Home Depot lol

Heyyyy!

(Yawning) Oh, man! I'm just waking up from my nap. And Like one of my sisters said, these meds are not only for the pain but for the "rest" that my body needs, and I agree. (Cause Dr. H looked at me in disbelief when I told him I was already tryna do work.)

But anyhow, guess what y'all??? I saw Dr. C today, and before you stands, a woman with alllll clean margins!!! Meaning I made the right decision as far as the mastectomy cause the tissue was examined, and although there was a "tiny bit" of Cancer cells left in the affected area, we can now confirm for sure that the rest is **#Cancerfree**.

Hallelujaaaaaaah! Thank you, Jesus!! So as he said to me,

there's no need anymore for us to see each other again unless I need him for something else or we just so happen to bump into each other at **HOME DEPOT**.

Awwww... leaving him is sooo bittersweet; he's sooo awesome. I highly recommend him. And to think he left me a message last week to tell me the good news. But I was a bit afraid and like I told him today... I needed to hear this face to face from you.

And he said to me, "I love you! You're a 'can-do person.' One who'll spread the gospel and let others know that yes, life is not a bed of roses, but you can do it!"

I love my surgeon, y'all.

And to think I was sooo excited that I forgot to take our picture. **AGAIN**.

But it's okay cause thanks to Mrs. Kathy, I gotta go back for his brochures.

OMG LINA!!!! THAT'S GOOD NEWS...DOES THIS MEAN YOU'RE DONE???

Nahhh, I wish! I still gotta do radiation (the extra icing on the cake), finish my recon (which, BTW, he's so pleased with Dr. H's work), and complete my adjunct treatment with Dr. K (which is the preventative plan she's putting me on for five to ten years). But surgically, they're done! Bye-bye Cancer.

Sooo today, April 17, is another Cancerversary for me. The day my surgeon said, "we've got alllll clear margins."

Cleannnn, y'alll. Cleeaaaan!!!! Clean, clean, clean!!!! Clean and healed in the mighty name of Jesus. Hallelujah, amen.

"My God is my Healer."
Psalm 30:2

"I have heard your prayer and seen your tears. I will heal you."
2 Kings 20:5 NIV

Declare today
"By His Stripes, I am Healed!"
Isaiah 53:5 NKJ

Then He said to her, "Daughter, your faith has healed you. Go in peace."
Luke 8:48 NIV

WEDNESDAY, APRIL 18
May I Add

One of the things I repeated as they wheeled me into the OR was, "I'm **HEALED**, I'm **HEALED**. I'm Cancer-free." So my word of encouragement for y'all is #Speak! #Speak! #Speak! And declare the promises of the Lord over your life. God is able. He is able to do all things abundantly, above and beyond all we could ever hope for. #AffirmIt.

Secondly, by being afraid to look at the pathology results, I kept myself a couple of days from the good news. But the thing is, I, too, must remind myself that when we **KNOW** that God is for us, what are we to fear?!! #ReallyTho.

Thirdly, my first sight as I walked home was my baby boy sleeping. It bothers me not being able to hold him for at least six weeks after surgery. But it brings me joy to know that I can now officially say, "I made it! I made it! I made it! I made it! because of His goodness I made it!

Friends,

Thank you so much for journeying with me from Cancer to **SURVIVA**.

My hope is that my testimony has not only empowered you but encouraged you to **BELIEVE**.

"But wait a minute, Lina, the truth is everyone won't be healed."

Oh, ye of little faith, don't even entertain it; just stand firm and **CLAIM IT**!

YOU CAN-CER VIVE this.

Love, Lina

Acknowledgments

Dream Team,
Riverside Peninsula Cancer Institute and Infusion Center Newport News, for WALKING WITH ME EVERY STEP OF THE WAY!

Pink Sisters,
Taneil Sanders, Shaneaka Felton, Kelli Virgil, and Blanca O'Brien; for fighting till the very, very end.

I Love You All.
This book is for you!

Love, Lina

The Journey Continues...

RADIATION.

www.ingramcontent.com/pod-product-compliance
Lightning Source LLC
Chambersburg PA
CBHW070840160426
43192CB00012B/2251